Hawai'i's Strangest Ickiest Wildest Book Ever!

Science, Natural History, Animals,
Hawaiian History, Island Trivia...
It's All Here and All So Disgusting,
You Won't Even Notice You're Learning!

Kathryn Drury Wagner

Mutual Publishing

ISBN: 978-1939487-12-4
Library of Congress Control Number: 2013947527
Design by Jane Gillespie

First Printing, October 2013

Mutual Publishing, LLC
1215 Center Street, Suite 210
Honolulu, Hawaii 96816
Ph: (808) 732-1709
Fax: (808) 734-4094
e-mail: info@mutualpublishing.com
www.mutualpublishing.com

Printed in Korea

To Kay Drury

Table of Contents

It came from the Deep 15

creepy crawlies 77

Acknowledgments

I wrote this book with my oldest daughter, Zoë, in mind, because she doesn't have a firm grasp on what I do for a living. Editing and writing, I keep explaining, but she seems to think I just go to yoga. Hopefully this book will give her a tangible example of my career—and provide her with gross-out fodder for many a sleepover to come.

I want to thank my husband, Brett, and other daughter, Delilah, for putting up with my shenanigans. My dear friend Lavonne Leong for pushing me to this project; my editor at Mutual Publishing, Jane Gillespie; and Sheila Sarhangi, for always being a wonderful sounding board.

Lastly, I thank my mother, Kay Drury, who was a biology teacher for decades and loves teaching young people—or people of any age, really—more than anyone I have ever known. To Mom, who can dissect a frog with one hand and eat a ham sandwich with the other.

Cockroaches

The roaches of Hawai'i are famous for two reasons: One, for their size, like the enormous "B-52" roaches. Second, the sheer number of roaches scurrying around in the Islands. This tends to freak out people from other places—Canadians run screaming—but people who live in Hawai'i are tough. We know roaches are just part of life. We whack them and we move on.

Still, everyone has at least one really good gross-out story they can tell about roaches. Want to hear mine? I once heated up some tea in the microwave, and after a minute on high, I opened the door. Inside were three roaches. Two were still moving. Which proves, I guess, that two out of three roaches can survive being zapped like leftovers. Yuck.

Hawai'i is home to nineteen kinds of cockroaches, but usually, we're dealing with three types: German (the small, fast brown ones), American (big buggahs with wings), and the Surinam, or "burrowing" roach, which mostly lives in yards, not inside houses.

What's on the Menu?

Cockroaches will eat anything, and I mean *anything!* ⇨   ⇨   ⇨   ⇨

Cockroaches can and will taste sleeping humans, taking a nip of eyelash, sampling a fingernail, or nibbling on hands and toenails. Infestations on ships sometimes got so bad, sailors had to wear gloves before they went to bed. Cockroaches sure put the omni in omnivore, that's for sure!

Menu

Cheese
Leather
Pet food
Hair
Dry skin
Other insects (live or dead)
Each other
Book bindings
Toothpaste
Wallpaper paste
Ladies' nylon Stockings
Old rice
Dead mice
Peanuts
Fish
Boots
Glue off a postage stamp
Houseplants

Headless Wonder

These buggahs are hard to kill. A cockroach can live for up to six weeks without food, two weeks without water and a month without…its head. A decapitated human would quickly bleed to death, but not a roach. They have a different kind of circulation system than we do, with less blood pressure. A human also needs a brain to move around, but that's not how roaches work. They have nerves throughout their whole body that can control it, even without a brain.

But how would the roach breathe without a nose and mouth? Roaches breathe through little holes in their bodies.

What happens to a headless roach? It can live for a few weeks up to a month. Gradually, it will dry out and die. Or, mold will grow on it, and then it will die.

Hmm. How about the opposite: Can a roach head live without the body? Yep.

As long as the head is fed and kept cool, it can survive for days. No wonder roaches are so hard to get rid of!

Roaches, Roaches, Everywhere

For every one roach you spot, there are a hundred other roaches you aren't seeing. Roaches are mostly nocturnal; if you see them during the day, that means there are a whole lot of roaches around.

Did You Know?

Roaches stink. No, literally. They give off a strong odor. Sometimes if a place is really infested, you'll be able to smell an awful, oily scent.

Why are Roaches Bad?

Besides being just plain old nasty, cockroaches have bacteria and germs on their feet. After all, they have traveled through some pretty gross places, like sewers and drain pipes and crawl spaces. They drag those germs into our houses (thanks, guys!). They can also contaminate our food by shedding. And, they leave their poop, which looks like coffee or ground pepper, all over the place.

Did You Know?

Roaches are cold blooded, so they need a lot less food than you or I do. If they had to, they could last up to a month without eating a meal. I can't even skip lunch!

All in the family!

Cockroaches and termites share a common ancestor: A bug that lived 300 million years ago. They are also related to the preying mantis.

They Shed

We have our bones on the inside of our bodies, but roaches have an exoskeleton, a skeleton on the outside. It's that crunchy shell-like layer. As the roach grows, it needs more room to stretch, so it sheds its exoskeleton. They do this about six to twelve times over their lives.

For about eight hours after it sheds, the roach will look white, and then it will start to turn back to its normal color. The thrown-out exoskeleton of the roach dries out and decays, becoming tiny flakes. These get puffed into the air and guess who breathes them in? *Us*. This is actually one of the causes of asthma, which makes it hard for kids to breathe. Another good reason to avoid having roaches around.

Their Senses are Different

Hearing, taste, touch, sight and smell—roaches have the same five senses we do. But they are set up in weird ways:

- You have a nose...they can smell things using their antennae.
- You have ears...they hear by feeling vibrations with their feet.
- Your mouth goes up and down when you chew...a roach's mouth goes sideways.
- You touch with your fingers...a roach feels safe when it's being touched from all sides, like if it's in a small crevice in the wall. They are more nervous out in the open.
- Your eyes have one lens each...a roach has compound eyes, with 2,000 lenses.

Roaches as Pets

Did You Know?

People who keep cockroaches as pets are called fanciers. They like to collect the more exotic, tropical roaches, and keep them in an aquarium tank. Some people think they make good pets, because they don't need a lot of space and are interesting to watch. If you have a roach as a pet, you can give it toilet-paper tubes and egg cartons to hide under, and feed it oats, fruit and even dog or cat food. Unlike a dog, you don't have to walk them with a leash! And unlike a cat, roaches cannot be trained to use a litter box. Here are some types enthusiasts like. They have funny names!

Hissing roach

Fake Death's Head roach

True Death's Head roach
(Will the real Death's Head roach please stand up?)

Giant Cave roach

Ornate Velvet roach

Peppered roach

Australian Rhino roaches

Tiger Hissers

Orange-head roach

© Dmstudio | Dreamstime.com

This is So Gross

Edward Archbold, age thirty-two, died after a roach-eating contest. He ate dozens of roaches for an October 2012 "Midnight Madness" event, then threw up and collapsed. Doctors later found he had choked to death on the roach body parts.

"That's a big insect," a bug expert named Bill Kern told the local paper, the *Miami Herald*. "When you bite into it, you're going to get a gush of fat bodies, the gut content and the hemolymph—essentially insect blood. As you bite down, that's going to put pressure on the exoskeleton, so when it's ruptured, it's going to squirt." Kern also told the *Herald* that the legs of the roaches are "covered with pretty stout spines, that could irritate the esophagus and stomach, in addition to the crunchy, leathery, paper-like wings you have to chew up."

What's the moral of this story? Do not eat a bucketful of roaches.

© Fwhb | Dreamstime.com

Gotta Motor

→ The American cockroach has wings, but doesn't really flap around and fly—it just kind of glides from point to point. That's why they seem to be dive-bombing us.

→ Roaches can run up to three miles an hour.

→ If a human could sprint the same way a roach moves, we'd go up to 200 miles an hour.

→ Roaches have six legs and eighteen knees.

→ They can turn their bodies twenty-five times in one second.

→ Climbing walls is easy for them, because their feet have little tiny claws built in.

→ Males weigh less and can run faster than females.

→ For all their speed, roaches are actually really lazy. They spend seventy-five percent of their time resting. (Probably daydreaming about new ways to gross us humans out.)

© Roy Chang

What's That Stuff?

When you step on a roach or smack it with your slippah, the white goo that squirts out is their blood. A female roach will sometimes have orange blood.

Now, let's say you didn't move fast enough, and you hit the roach with a glancing blow. You only whacked off one roach leg. The roach will live without the leg until the next time it molts, when the leg will gradually start to regrow.

Eyewitness

"I'd seen a few roaches around the toaster, so I went to clean out the crumbs. I discovered the roaches were LIVING in the toaster, and when I dumped it out, I counted seventeen of them—some alive, some dead." —Kathy

The Roach Express

Roaches took over a Greyhound bus in March of 2013. The bus was about fifteen minutes into the trip from Atlantic City, New Jersey, to New York City, when suddenly, roaches started pouring out of the air vents. "People were in the aisles literally brushing roaches off of them," a passenger told news channel CNN. "Roaches started crawling up on our clothes, falling down from the ceiling." The driver pulled the bus over, everyone got off and the company sent a new bus to pick up the passengers.

Roaches also enjoy flying on planes. In 2011, a North Carolina couple sued an airline after cockroaches crawled out of the air vents, causing "great distress to a number of passengers."

And boats, sure! Why not? The famous ship HMS *Bounty* was so overrun with roaches, cranky Captain Bligh demanded it to be completely cleaned with boiling water before it could be used again. Another famous sea captain, Sir Francis Drake, once captured a ship, only to find it crawling with millions of roaches. I bet he wanted to give *that* ship back!

Eyewitness

"I walked into the bathroom, flipped on the light, and saw that there was this big roach, sitting right on top of my toothbrush!" —Kay

© Margouillat | Dreamstime.com and © Konstantin | Dreamstime.com

Myth or Fact?

Could a cockroach really survive a nuclear bomb? Well, they are really good at shoving themselves into small cracks and crevices, which might give them a fighting chance. And they are unusually tolerant of radiation. They can stand sixteen times as much as humans can. But, at the center of a nuclear bomb, it's ten million degrees Celsius. So a roach would be cooked instantly.

Zombie Roaches!

The Emerald Cockroach Wasp is about an inch long, and a shiny, metallic green. It's kind of pretty, and it lives in Hawai'i. But it doesn't act pretty. Get this: When a female emerald cockroach wasp is ready to lay an egg, she finds herself a cockroach. She stings it one time—right in the middle of its body—with a venom. This venom makes the roach's front legs collapse. Then boom! She stings the roach again, stabbing right into its brain! She pokes around with her stinger, finds a special part of the roach's brain, and injects a venom into that area. Soon, the roach's legs recover, and it can walk again. But it's a zombie roach. Its brain has been changed by the wasp's venom and now, it lacks the desire to escape.

Next, the wasp—I hope you're sitting down—grabs the roach's antennae, bites off the tips and drinks what is inside. Then the wasp pulls the roach along, just like you would a little dog on a leash, and leads it away. She brings it to her burrow, and then lays her egg on the roach's body (remember, the roach doesn't know it should be running away from this horrible situation). She plugs up the hole to her nest with small rocks, and takes off.

Poor zombie roach just stays in the burrow, for five weeks, not eating or drinking. The wasp egg hatches, and the larva that was inside the egg chews a hole through the side of the roach. It starts to grow inside the still-alive roach. (No, I am not making this up.) It slowly eats its way through the roach's organs—nibble, nibble. Then it makes a cocoon inside the roach's now-empty body. When it's ready to be a grown-up wasp, it breaks out of the roach, and heads out of the burrow. Zombified. Buried alive. Eaten while you can't move. This is so awful, it almost makes you feel bad for cockroaches.

© Roy Chang

How to kill a Roach

So assuming you don't want these repulsive creatures in your house, what can you do?

❶ Get a gecko. They love to grind on 'ono roaches.

❷ Or a cat. Some cats will chase and kill roaches, but most are too lazy to be bothered.

❸ Mash them with heavy objects like books or rolled up magazines.

❹ Smack them with the Islands' weapon of choice: A slippah.

❺ Roach baits. Here's how they work. A roach eats some of the poison, crawls back to the nest, and dies. The other roaches eat him and they die, too. More roaches might get killed by the poison in roach spit and roach poop that's in their nest. Nice!

❻ Mix sugar and baking soda together and leave it out for them to eat. The roach will eat the sugar because it's sweet, and the baking soda will bubble in them, messing up their stomachs and eventually killing them.

❼ A thing called diatomaceous earth cuts the roach's exoskeleton. They'll dry out and die.

❽ Boric acid. The roach crawls over the powder and the sharp crystals of the boric acid get trapped in the joints of their legs. It cuts them; they lose water and dry out and die.

❾ Sticky traps, otherwise known as Hoy Hoy traps or Roach Motels. "Roaches check in but they never check out."

❿ Spraying them with soap and water. The soap blocks the holes in their body and they suffocate. Most Hawai'i roaches would laugh in the face of this idea, I think. They might just ask you for a washcloth.

⓫ Flush them.

⓬ In cold places, wait for winter. Roaches freeze at temperatures lower than thirty-two degrees.

⓭ A professional exterminator.

Hissing Roaches

Here's a fun kind of roach: *Gromphadorhina* is known for making a hissing sound. It's loud enough to scare the family dog!

Eyewitness

"Once I bought a car for a very low price; it seemed too good to be true. At night I was driving and noticed several roaches, so I put three bug bombs in it and rolled up all the windows. The next morning I aired the car out and started the dirty deed of vacuuming up the roaches. To my surprise, I had to empty the dust buster three times—there were hundreds of dead nasty critters!" —Jessee

How to Trap a Roach

Use a bowl with steep sides and lightly rim the sides with petroleum jelly. The slippery jelly will keep them from being able to climb out once they go into the bowl. As bait, put banana slices, carrot bits, or hunks of bread or potato in the bowl. Place it out at night, in a moist spot, like the bathroom. If you want to make it even easier for the roach to come inside the bowl, you can build a little ramp up to the bowl with a paper towel.

Oh Mama

A mother roach only has to mate once, and she stays pregnant the rest of her life, continuing to lay eggs. They lay a pouch of eggs, attaching the egg case to something like a cardboard box, using their saliva. Roaches don't lay one egg a time, like a chicken, but a whole bunch at once. That means a single roach can have up to 1,400 babies!

Pali Highway © Chee-onn Leong | Dreamstime.com

Eyewitness

"I had a roach crawl across my face when we were driving. I had to pull over on the Pali. And oh, I hate finding their weird bean-looking poop on my clean, folded sheets in my closet!" —Sheila

Eyewitness

"We just got back from Maui. We had a rental car that was infested with cockroaches. They came pouring our of the backseat as we drove down the road. My son jumped into the front with us, and we stopped at the first store we came to. Used a whole can of Raid in the car, and then locked it up overnight. No more bugs in the car." —Nancy, on Fodors' travel forum

Cockroach Racing

▶▶ Australia has an annual cockroach race, "The greatest gathering of thoroughbred cockroaches in the world." Inside a twenty-foot ring, the contestant roaches are let out of their bottles. Whichever roach gets to the edge of the ring first is declared winner.

▶▶ Every four years, there's a Presidential Cockroach Derby, held in New Jersey. Two giant roaches—one for the Republican and one for the Democrat—race across a three-foot track. Supposedly, whichever roach wins will predict who becomes the next U.S. President.

▶▶ A college in Maryland has an annual "Running of the Roaches," where roaches compete in both marathons and sprints.

Bet You Didn't Know This...

Roaches have gizzards! They grind their food with it and then swallow.

Eyewitness

"Roach parts—bits of legs— were coming out of the water cooler at work. We pulled up the water jug, and there were three roaches inside the tank." —Lori

Or This...

The reason roaches are so hard to catch is that they have delicate hairs on their back ends. The hairs sense air motion—like you, raising up your shoe to smack him—and the roach can leap out of the way.

When do roaches sleep

They sleep a lot during the day and are more active at night. Roaches are only active for about four hours per day.

Eyewitness

"A first glance at the pillow showed me ... cockroaches as large as peach leaves—fellows with long, quivering antennae and fiery, malignant eyes ... shortly thereafter a procession of cockroaches arrived and camped in my hair. I was beginning to feel really annoyed. I got up and put my clothes on and went up on deck."

—famous writer Mark Twain

© Roy Chang

Roaches as a Snack

Feeling like an adventure? Some cultures eat bugs, which are good sources of protein, calcium and iron. You can buy deep-fried cockroaches in Thailand and Cambodia. Or, you can taste some at the Explorer's Club dinners in New York City, where diners chew on things like rattlesnake, camel, fried cod head, and cockroaches on a stick.

Robo-Roaches

Scientists have been able to control the movements of roaches by putting small backpacks onto them and zapping them lightly with electricity. The "Robo-Roaches" are controlled using a joystick. This idea may someday be used to help find people trapped in earthquakes, because the Robo-Roaches can crawl into very small, tight spaces with a camera.

Eyewitness

In the fall of 2012, roaches swarmed by the thousands into a neighborhood in 'Ewa Beach on O'ahu. 'Ewa Wai Gentry. A bug expert says they were Pacific beetle roaches. People who lived there could easily fill a whole jar with roaches in just one day. The roaches were in yards, in people's driveways, crawling over the sides of their house and yes, coming inside. No one knows why the roaches suddenly multiplied.

Roaches in the Arts

There's a play called *The Fate of a Cockroach*. It was put on at UCLA, where students spent two months making elaborate cockroach costumes. They also wore masks and long red antennae. The play takes place in a bathroom, so the set was a big bar of soap and part of a bathtub.

If you'd rather read a scary book about roaches, P.J. Neri wrote a book, *Hawai'i Chillers No.6: Killer Cockroaches*. The roaches in her book have mutated due to a pesticide. Now six feet tall, they hide in a sugar mill, plotting to take over the world.

© Roy Chang

Say It, Don't Spray It

A species found in Hawai'i, *Diploptera punctata*, sprays a nasty fluid from its abdomen if it's attacked. This helps it avoid being eaten by a hungry rodent. I'm guessing the rat is probably not amused to be sprayed in the face.

Chocolate-Covered Roach

Most people who are allergic to chocolate aren't really allergic to chocolate. They are allergic to the tiny, ground-up pieces of cockroaches *in* the chocolate. About eight insect parts are found in the chocolate bars, reports ABC News. But no worries… Anything less than sixty bits of insect per one hundred grams of chocolate is considered safe. Ugh! Cockroach particles are found in lots of foods, like peanut butter, popcorn, wheat, fruit and cheese.

© Roy Chang

Even if you hate roaches, you have to give them some credit. They've been living on Earth for 350 million years and are found all over the planet—on every continent, except Antarctica—making them the most successful animal ever.

Eyewitness

"I found one crawling around next to the trash can last night, and instead of the obvious reaction of just stepping on it (I was wearing flip flops), I freaked out and went to the next room and grabbed one of my husband's huge work boots to squish it with. Two good squishes, and then took the trash out. I left it there last night, under the giant boot, to teach it a lesson. And it was really gross, and I didn't want to look at again for fear it might move or something.

I went to go vacuum it up this morning, and it was gone! All that was there was a leg or two, a wing, and an antenna.. And then I saw it! Moving! Alive! So I squished it again! This boot weighs like seven pounds; I don't understand how it survived.

Before I could go get the vacuum, [my chicken] Chickpea came in and ate it. I'm very grateful that she took care of it for me, but I don't know if I can pet her again knowing there is a squashed roach inside of her." —Posted on BackYard Chickens.com

Chapter Two

It Came from the Deep

The ocean is so big and so deep, it's almost like it's another planet. That's why humans are still discovering new things about the ocean. No one had gotten photos of a giant squid swimming, for example, until recently. The ocean is home to amazing—and odd—creatures. Some glow, some will sting you, some shoot water out of their tushes. Hey, whatever works. There are animals that can change color, or even go from being a boy to a girl. Slimy, gooey, prickly, puffy—you name it, and there's a sea creature that fits the bill. It's a wild world down there. And sometimes, those creatures come up to the surface... Let's take a look and see what we can find.

Cone Shell Mollusk

Such a pretty shell! But be careful—the cone shell mollusk is one nasty little critter. Sure, they look like slow moving, sweet little snails, but cone shell mollusks are actually fast and deadly. They have venom glands and use their bodies' tiny harpoons to strike out at anyone who is trying to eat them, like an octopus. They can also use their venom and barb to attack their own prey, so they can eat. They like to eat smaller fish and worms.

To eat a fish, first, the mollusk stings it to paralyze it. Then it grabs onto the fish with one long tooth—ew—and gloms on, waiting until the venom takes effect and the fish stops breathing. Then it consumes the fish whole. Yikes.

This venom is dangerous to humans, too, and it can kill a person within only five minutes. If you see a cone shell, leave it right where it is and don't touch it.

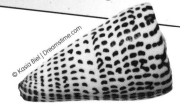

Box Jelly Fish © Daleen Loest | Dreamstime.com

Box Jelly-fish

- He sees you when you're swimming; he knows when you're awake... A box jellyfish has twenty-four eyes, grouped around the four sides of its squishy, bell-shaped body. What it's doing with these eyes, no one knows. Because *it has no brain.*

- Also called the Sea Wasp, *Chironex fleckeri* is so venomous, it's one of the most dangerous animals on Earth. Lucky we live Hawai'i, because that type of box jellies only live in the ocean around Australia. But we do have our own kind of box jellies.

- How do they sting? All along their tentacles, box jellyfish have little triggers that release tiny, stinging threads. So if you brush against a jellyfish while you're swimming in the ocean, that's what hits your skin and gives you a painful, burning feeling. A sting from a box jellyfish can cause people to go into shock, the place where you got stung can hurt for weeks. A dead jellyfish's tentacles can sting just as well as a live one, so be careful if you come across a dead jellyfish on the beach.

- They have no skeleton, heart, brain or head, but box jellyfish have sixty, count 'em, sixty, "anal regions." That's a lot of rear end!

© Roy Chang

Cushion Star (Also known as "Slime Stars")

Cushion stars are a type of starfish covered in thick, slimy mucus. It's to keep other animals from eating them.

They're so gooey, you wouldn't want to keep one in your fish tank. They can clog an aquarium filter.

This starfish eats by sticking its stomach outside of its body and digesting what it touches. If you bother it while it's eating, it will quickly yank its stomach back inside.

Cushion Star © John P. Hoover

© Roy Chang

Flying Fish © Jamen Percy | Dreamstime.com

Flying Fish

A flying fish shoots out of the water at thirty-seven miles an hour! Well, it's not actually flying—they don't have wings. Flying fish are using their special fins to zoom up to four feet in the air, and can glide up to 655 feet. They can get up so high; people often find them inside of their boats.

Eel

The Hawaiian word for eel is puhi, and there are eighty species of moray eel in Hawai'i.

Did You Know?

◎ Eels like to hide in crevices in the reef, and are usually nocturnal. That means you aren't likely to see them during the day. At night, they will come out of their safe spots to hunt for dinner: octopus, fish and crabs.

◎ The viper moray has large, sharp teeth—so large, it can't close its mouth. Still, eels aren't usually aggressive to humans and only bite when they are surprised. Snorkelers or divers who accidentally step on them, or people who poke their fingers into an eel's hiding spot, will get bitten.

◎ The yellow margin eel is considered fiercer. They will leave their rocky hiding spot to check out the catch of a spearfisherman.

◎ Eels that feed on fish have teeth that curve backward to make swallowing the fish easier. Eels that eat crabs have smooth teeth, like cobblestones, that can grind up shells.

◎ Most are two feet long, but a moray can grow up to five feet long.

◎ Their flesh is toxic.

◎ If you see an eel opening and closing its mouth, don't worry—that's just how they breathe.

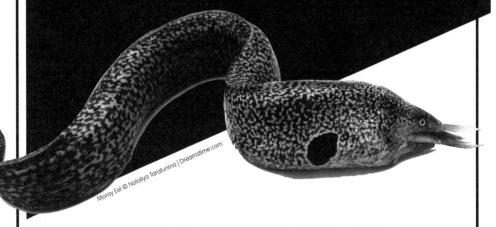

Moray Eel © Nataliya Taratunina | Dreamstime.com

Giant Squid

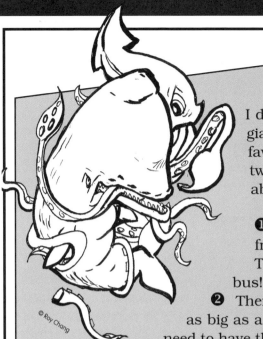

© Roy Chang

I don't know about you, but giant squid are one of my favorite animals. Here are twenty mind-blowing facts about these rubbery beasts:

❶ They grow anywhere from thirty to forty feet. That's as long as a school bus!

❷ Their eyes are huge—about as big as a soccer or volleyball. They need to have these big, dinner-plate-size eyes so they can spot things in the dark water where they live.

❸ They live deep under the ocean, at 1,650 to 3,300 feet. To give you a sense how far that is, that's like if you climbed up Diamond Head... four times. It's pretty far! And it's freezing cold and pitch black down there.

❹ Because they stay down so deep in the water, giant squid are very mysterious. Before 2004, no one had gotten pictures of a live one swimming. The only things we knew about this animal came from studying the bodies of dead squid, which sometimes wash up on beaches or float to the surface of the ocean.

❺ Giant squid are found in all the oceans of the world. The waters around Hawai'i are a little too warm for their comfort, but they occasionally will come by for a visit. A giant squid was caught ten miles off O'ahu in 1981. A twenty-five-footer was picked up off Kailua-Kona by *Illusions*, a sport fishing boat. That squid was missing a big chunk of its body, like it had recently lost a battle with a shark.

❻ They start off life quite small: They are only .125 inches long as babies. That's like the margin on this page!

❼ Giant squid grow incredibly fast. They don't live long—typically two to three years—so squid have to sprout into adult size really quickly. If human babies grew at the same pace as a giant squid, we'd be 8,000 feet tall by the time we were three years old!

BONUS SQUID FACT #1
One type of squid, the Hawaiian bobtail, glows like it's a night-light. The glow actually comes from bacteria, not batteries.

❽ Tipping the scales at 440 pounds is about average for a giant squid.

❾ A giant squid is the cousin of the colossal squid; they are not the same thing.

❿ What's on the menu? Giant squid eat smaller squid and fish. To grab their prey, they use their eight arms (with suckers on them) and two long tentacles, also studded with suckers. The tentacles can grab food that's thirty-three feet away. That's the length of a motor home. Can you imagine sitting on your couch and reaching your arms into your next-door neighbor's fridge for a snack?

⓫ Sperm whales eat them. We know this because scientists find leftover, undigested squid beaks in the stomachs of sperm whales. Burp!

⓬ Giant squid don't have tongues like ours. They have a radula; it's like a tongue covered in teeth.

⓭ They are not tasty. "It was really awful," said Dr. Clyde Roper, a squid expert at the Smithsonian who once tasted cooked giant squid. Guess that rules out the idea of a giant pile of calamari…

⓮ Do you want to see a giant squid? There are twelve dead giant squids on display at museums throughout the world, kept in tanks filled with preservatives so they won't dry out or decay.

Hawaiian Bobtail Squid © John P. Hoover

15 Their brains are shaped like a donut.

16 A giant squid's esophagus—that's the tube leading from its mouth to its stomach—runs straight through the hole in the brain. Guess you could say they have food on their minds!

17 Female giant squid are always bigger than the males.

18 The giant squid's scientific name, *Architeuthis dux*, means "most important squid leader." Yes, sir!

19 There are 500 types of squid in the world's oceans. The smallest are only an inch long.

20 Longest title of a book about squid? A Danish scientist wrote *Hectoctyldannelsen hos Octopodslaegterne Argonauta og Tremoctopus, oplyst ved Iagttagelse af lignende Dannelser hos Blacksprutterne i Almindelighed.* Phew! That's a mouthful.

> ### BONUS SQUID FACT #2
> In Hawaiian mythology, there's a squid god named Kakahe'e. He lived near Ka'ena Point in a sea cave.

Lionfish

Cranky and poisonous, this is one fish you don't want to snuggle up to. Their sharp fins contain venom—and they have plenty of options for poking you, because they can use their dorsal, anal or pelvic spines. The venom is not fatal to humans, but it's extremely painful. Adding to the fun, the spine can break off inside your wound. Ouch.

Hawaiian Red Lionfish © John P. Hoover

Lionfish eat just about everything and are always hungry. If they come across a big meal, no problem: their stomachs can expand up to thirty times the normal size. Lionfish are invading oceans around the world, multiplying too quickly.

BURP!

© Roy Chang

FUN FACT

Ever wonder what whale poop looks like? When whales "drop a deuce," it's hard to miss! You'll see a huge orange or reddish cloud in the water. "An oceanic skid mark the size of two Volvos," as one observer put it. The cloud in the water is made up of stinky blobs of whale poop, each about the size of your hand, that float to the surface. And no, whales do not use toilet paper.

"Thar she.. poops!"

© Roy Chang

Banded Ribbon Worm © John P. Hoover

Marine Worms

Bet you didn't know these worm tidbits:

- The parchment worm catches food using sticky mucus bags. And if it feels scared, it casts off mucus that glows.
- Ribbon worms have barbs that they use to stab other worms.
- If its head gets cut off, an acorn worm can regrow its head within a few days. And if you touch it, it will stain your hands an icky brown color because of a chemical in its skin.
- A divided flatworm is both a boy worm AND a girl worm.

oarfish

Most fish swim sideways, but not oarfish. These huge fish can swim with their head up, tail down. They can also swim on their side, like most fish do, when they want to. They are pretty mysterious, because they are deepwater fish and rarely seen alive. But if you found a dead one washed up on a beach, you'd see a silver fish, ten- to fifty-feet long, topped with a reddish crest. No wonder people used to believe in sea serpents!

In case you were hoping to make a really long piece of sushi, oarfish have gel-like flesh and aren't considered edible.

Also answers to: "The King of the Herrings." Well, excuse us!

Manta Ray © J. Henning Buchholz | Dreamstime.com

Manta Rays

Graceful manta rays are big, but they won't hurt you. They don't have stinging barbs on them, and though they are close relatives of sharks, they don't have any teeth. They just inhale their food—plankton and tiny crabs—by sucking it in whole. They can grow from twenty-two to thirty feet wide, and weigh up to 3,000 pounds. When it's born, a baby manta already weighs twenty pounds!

Mysterious Purple crabs

In the summer of 2012, tiny purple invaders overran the south shore of O'ahu. The little crabs were only about the size of a berry, but there were *millions* of them. Scientists think they were young Seven Eleven crabs—not the place you buy a musubi; the name of the crabs is Seven Eleven. Also called a spotted reef crab, these baby crabs will grow into an adult size of up to six inches across. They were mostly likely washed in by Hurricane Daniel, which passed near the Islands.

Needlefish

Imagine this. You're night diving with your flashlight. The next thing you know, a slim fish, about four feet long, swims up to you and impales you with its super-sharp snout. Ouch! Needlefish attacks on people are rare, but often fatal. These fish have been called a "living javelin" because they are so sharp and speedy—they can swim up to thirty-seven miles an hour.

A man spearfishing off Kahana Bay on Oʻahu was attacked by a needlefish and wound up needing multiple stitches, surgery on his liver and a week at The Queen's Medical Center. Another man was paddling his one-man canoe when a needlefish leapt out the water and jabbed him in the knee. He had to have a four-inch cut by a surgeon to get out all the fish's jaw, which was stuck in his leg. These fish don't fool around.

If you're in a fishing boat, you're not safe from these guys either. Needlefish swim along in the water close to the surface; light from a boat attracts and excites them, causing them to leap right into the boat. A boy on Kauaʻi was night fishing with his father when a fish jumped out the water and stabbed him through the skull, killing him. Maybe we should add helmets as part of our fishing gear?

© Roy Chang

Crocodile Needlefish © John P. Hoover

Octopus

The most common kind of octopus in Hawai'i is the eight-armed day octopus, or he'e. Do you want to learn more about these cool creatures?

First of all, they have a weird body.

* An octopus has three hearts and blue blood.
* It can't hear, but it has great eyesight.
* And the nearly 2,000 suction cups on its arms—lined up in two rows—are able to smell and taste, so it can find food easily. It grabs the food with its arms, jumps on top and eats it with its sharp beak.
* An octopus has no bones, but is almost all muscle—making them really strong.
* If an octopus loses an arm, it can grow a new one.

Awww. Sort of. A mother octopus will guard her eggs for four to six weeks on the ocean floor, never leaving them. She will slowly starve to death and when she dies, her body provides food for her young.

The escape artist. An octopus can change colors to blend into its background, and even change its texture—bumpy, ridged—to look just like its surroundings. It can squirt water at predators, will hold up rocks to protect itself and as a last resort, it will release ink. The ink can hide the octopus as it escapes or even temporarily blind a fish.

Short-arm Sand Octopus © John P. Hoover

Parrotfish

A girl parrotfish can change to become a boy parrotfish. And those super-strong jaws they use to chomp on coral are actually fused teeth. Crunch!

Peacock flounder

The Case of the Roving Eyeball... Was solved by Mr. Peacock Flounder, on the ocean floor.

Take a look inside the case file: When peacock flounder are young, their eyes are on either side of their head—the way most fish are set up. But adult peacock flounder have both eyes on the same side. This allows them to cozy into the sand, flat on the bottom of the ocean, and blend in with both eyes looking upward.

Wait, so who moved the eye?

It was Mother Nature. As the flounder grow up, they go from swimming like a normal fish, to leaning to one side, and—get this!—one eye gradually moves to the other side of the fish's body. There are right-eyed, and left-eyed flounder, depending on which eye did the shift. Dah-dah-daaaaah! The plot thickens.

Panther Flounder © John P. Hoover

A giant, foot-long salp was found in a fishermen's net in 1956 in Hawai'i. They are usually only one to four inches long.

Salps

Is it a jellyfish? A clear sack of goo? What the heck? It's a salp. This gooey little guy is actually more complicated than a jellyfish: when it's a baby, it has a nerve cord, tails and gills. As it gets older, it loses those features and looks like...well, no offense, but it's slime with an eye. Salps move around by pumping water through their bodies; it's also how they eat. But here's where it gets gross. They make a little feeding net of mucus inside their bodies. Plankton gets stuck in the mucus net and moves to the animal's stomach.

Now, if there's a lot of plankton around, salps will pig out, sometimes eating so much food, they get clogged up and sink down into the ocean to their deaths. A lucky salp will remember to bud off a clone of itself while it's eating. Imagine this: You sat down to a huge plate lunch, realized you couldn't eat it all, so zoop! Out of your arm comes a new sister to help you chow down.

Salps don't sting or bite, but they can cause problems by gunking up fishing nets. They like to hang together in groups of up to a hundred, and they can get so heavy, the fishing nets rip. In 2012, salps clogged the pipes at a nuclear power plant in California, and workers had to temporarily shut it down. That's a lot of goo!

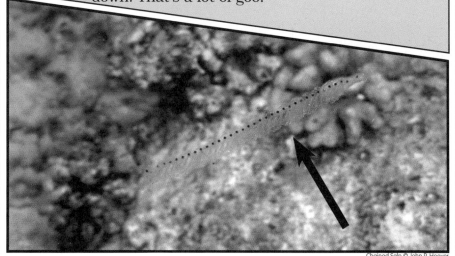

Chained Salp © John P. Hoover

Sea Anemones

They look so pretty, like colorful flowers swaying in the ocean. But watch out! This relative of the jellyfish is a fierce meat eater. Does the sea anemone buy steak at Foodland? No. It is a marine creature and besides, it is *way* too small to steer a shopping wagon. So it waits on a rock in the water, gently waving its tentacles around, pretending to be all innocent, until a small fish swims by. Then *wham!* The anemone stings it with a tentacle. The poor little fish is paralyzed and gets shoved, whole, into the sea anemone's mouth.

While we're too big to get eaten by a sea anemone, they will sting us if we step on them or get too close while swimming. A sting might cause oozing blisters, reddened skin, and pain that lasts for weeks.

Crazy fact:
One type of crab, called Lybia, has special claws that allow it to carry two small anemones around with it—one in each claw—for protection. It's kind of like having your own personal set of stun guns.

Pleasing Anemone © John P. Hoover

Sea cucumbers

Though they look a little different—with long bodies and leathery skin, these animals are related to starfish and sea urchins. Here's what you need to know about them:

Butt seriously. Sea cucumbers breathe by moving water in and out of their anus. They suck in the water, get the oxygen they need, and squirt it back out. Up to four cups of water an hour goes in and out!

Butt really?! They also get extra food this way; they have a mouth, but they get a little extra nutrition from what's being swooshed through their rear ends (I told you this was a gross-out book. You were warned!)

Butt it gets worse. Tiny animals, like worms, pearl fish and crabs, get sucked up into the sea cucumber's tush and stay, enjoying it as a little hidey hole. They come out at night to feed on the ocean floor.

Butt surely you are joking! Sea cucumbers can shoot their internal organs out of their butt. Some scientists think this is a way to defend themselves against predators; others think they do it just to clean themselves out. I don't know about you, but I would NOT want to eat some animal that is shooting its guts out of its rear end. I'm just saying.

© Roy Chong

Self Defense

In Hawaiian waters, sea cucumbers come in all sizes, from cute cukes only three inches long to whoppers up to fourteen inches in size.

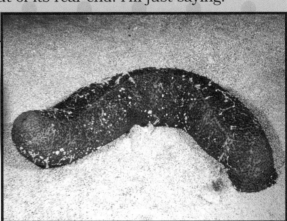

Paradoxical Sea Cucumber © John P. Hoover

Weird Sea Cuke facts:

➲ Sea cucumbers can change their bodies, becoming very firm, or very soft, when they want to. People can't do that; we have bones and lack the special connective tissue sea cucumbers have.

➲ In some types of sea cucumbers, even a small amount of leftover body can regrow a whole new sea cucumber.

➲ China has a thriving business in farming sea cucumbers, growing them in ponds or pens. Sea cucumbers are high in protein, and low in fat. Here's how they are prepared for markets, where they are sold dried. First, you take out the guts. Then you boil the sea cucumber and salt it. Then you boil it again and dry it out in the sun. Box it up and you're good to go.

Sea Horses

They are often seen floating vertically, with their heads up, but sea horses swim the fastest when they are horizontal.

Unlike humans, male sea horses are the ones who carry the babies, not the ladies.

Smooth Seahorse © John P. Hoover

Sea Slugs

These mollusks have bodies like snails, but don't wear a shell. "Huge shell-less wads of mucus; they feel like hunks of uncooked hamburger," reports Dr. Hans Bertsch, a marine biologist. One category of this animal is particularly crazy. It's called Nudibranchia (hee, hee.)

Pilsbry's Headshield Slug © John P. Hoover

That means "naked gills." Imagine a little blue guy, less than inch long, which looks like a squished gecko with extra legs.

- ✪ **Color me hungry.** Sea slugs come in a huge variety of body shapes and colors, and tend to match with their food. Red sea slugs dine on red sea sponges, for example, and even lay red eggs. It makes it harder for predators to spot them in the water.
- ✪ **Free Willy?** They are hermaphrodites, which means they have girl parts and boy parts. When they mate with another sea slug, the boy parts … well, they fall off. It's a detachable penis. But another one grows back in about a day.
- ✪ **Yum! Baked sea slug.** Ancient Hawaiians would cook sea slugs, which they called loli, in ovens. A chief on Maui loved it so much; the area he ruled became famous for it. People who lived there were teased, called 'ai loli (sea slug eaters).

Sea Urchins

They don't have brains or hearts—weird! These marine invertebrates do, however, have a few things going for them. One, they are tough and have venomous spines that can point in all directions. Second, they can move with their tiny tube feet. Unlike many animals, sea urchins have their mouths and five teeth on their underside, and they poop out of a hole on the top of their body.

Blue-Black Urchin © John P. Hoover

Sharks

There are forty kinds of sharks in Hawai'i. What's your favorite kind? It's so hard to choose! In the waters around Hawai'i you can find prickly sharks, frilled sharks, bluntnose sharks, bigeye thrasher sharks, even the rare megamouth sharks. How about the viper dogfish shark, the gulper shark, or the false cat shark? The sponge-headed cat shark sounds like it might clean a lot, while the cookie cutter shark makes me hungry because I start thinking about chocolate-chip cookies. Hey, try saying this one five times fast: shortspine spurdog shark.

Whoops!

Sharks have good vision, but they can make mistakes, occasionally biting submarines and underwater cables. It's true they sometimes bite humans, too, but it's rare—and it's a case of mistaken identity: they think we're a turtle or a sea lion. Humans don't even have enough fat on our meat for sharks to enjoy eating us.

Did You Know?

A megamouth shark's mouth has a mouth three feet across, even though the body is only 16 feet long. This rarely seen shark wasn't even discovered until 1976.

Chomp!

Cookie cutter sharks bite, then twist around, leaving a weird hole shape in their prey.

© Roy Chang

No salad bars: All sharks are carnivores. Some kinds of sharks eat seals, whales and dolphins, some eat fish, while others eat sea turtles, mollusks, clams, crab, squid and lobster. Sharks don't need to eat very often. They might not eat for weeks before getting hungry again.

Did You Know?

Sharks are ancient? They have been around for 400 million years! That's 200 million years older than dinosaurs. The biggest shark that ever lived, megalodon, was up to sixty feet long, and lived twenty-five to one-million years ago.

Yikes! You think you fight with your brother? Well, at least you didn't eat him. Because sandtiger sharks will eat a weaker sibling while they are still inside their mother's uterus.

Beep, beep... Hammerhead sharks move their heads back and forth along the ocean floor. They can find their prey using electric fields. Think of it like a shark metal detector, and it's right in their oddly-shaped head.

© Ian Scott | Dreamstime.com

Da-dum, da-dum: Forget movies like *Jaws*: there's no such thing as a "rogue shark" that's developed a taste for human flesh. You're more likely to die picking 'opihi or getting struck by lighting—both, I might add, are pretty rare—than you are to die from a fatal shark attack. Of all the kinds of sharks, 380, only three are considered dangerous: bull sharks, white sharks, and tiger shark. Bull sharks don't live in Hawai'i, white sharks are only rarely seen. That leaves tiger sharks, and even they don't bite humans very often. There are about seventy-five to one hundred shark attacks reported per year, and that's for the whole planet.

Uh, keep it inside your mouth, please?
Goblin sharks have jaws that can come out of their mouths.

Whack!
Thresher sharks use their unusually long tails to smack their prey, stunning their dinner so they can eat it.

A whale shark, the biggest species of shark, can grow to forty-five feet.

Some sharks lay eggs. Others give birth to live baby sharks, called pups. A shark's egg case is called a "mermaid's purse" or "devil's purse," and empty ones wash up onto the beach.

Fresh teeth: Shark teeth fall out all the time. Luckily, they have rows of new teeth coming up behind their old teeth. The smaller teeth push forward and the teeth in front fall out. It's like a tooth conveyor belt! A shark might create 30,000 teeth during its life.

BURP!

Did You Know?

These weird things have all been found in shark's stomachs:

❶ An old chicken coop, with leftover chicken bones and feathers.
❷ Shoes, an overcoat and a driver's license
❸ Chair
❹ The back end of a horse
❺ Torpedo
❻ Box of nails
❼ A missing sailor (alas, dead)
❽ Sixteenth century Portuguese medallion
❾ The remains of a polar bear
❿ Bag of potatoes

Smells good! A great white shark could smell a tiny, single drop of blood in an Olympic-size swimming pool.

Scorpionfish

Talk about being uncomfortable in your own skin! Twice a month, a leaf scorpionfish sheds its whole skin—just like snakes do. First, the skin around its head starts to split, then the rest comes off. Sometimes, the fish changes colors during this!

Shortsnout Scorpionfish © John P. Hoover

TWO-SIDED FISH

'Uko'a Fishpond in Waialua, Hawaiian legend goes, was home to strange fish. They would be part mullet and part weke, for example, or a mullet on one side and a weke on the other. They might be unusually fat or thin, and had bright colors that went deep into their bodies, even after they were scaled.

The Great Barracuda

Known as kaku in Hawaiian, this big, speedy fish can grow up to six feet long and one hundred pounds in weight. They have razor-sharp teeth, which they use to bite their prey in half—whoom!—before they circle back and chomp it into tiny morsels.

© Roy Chang

It's rare, but a barracuda will occasionally attack a human. It might see a sparkle in the water, such as a reflection off a hair barrette or a necklace, and think they are fish scales. A bite can be serious: one Maui fisherman needed 255 stitches to close up the wound on his leg after he was attacked by a barracuda. Worse, the barracudas' teeth can pull off, leaving embedded teeth in the wound. Ow. And all this time, I've been worried about shark bites.

Trumpetfish

Suck 'em up! Long, skinny trumpetfish hover upside down in the coral, waiting for smaller fish to swim by underneath. Then whoosh! It opens its mouth really wide, creating a powerful vacuum, and sucks the fish right in. It can do this because it has a special, stretchy mouth.

Tunicates

They look like pretty plants growing under the water, but these sack-shaped critters are undersea filter feeders. They pump water through their bodies, and pull out the plankton in the water to eat. They have some funny other names they also go by: sea squirt, sea pork, sea pineapple, sea grape, and sea tulip. Here are some freaky facts about them:

- Their blood is pale green.
- Every few minutes, their hearts stop beating. Then the heart starts pumping again, pushing in the opposite direction.
- U-shaped tummy.
- People in Japan and Korea eat the sea pineapple as food.
- Some types build a mucous net around themselves that they use as their house.
- They are hermaphrodites. They have girl parts AND boy parts.
- If they get scared, they shoot out water—that's why they are called "squirts."
- As a baby tunicate grows up, it undergoes metamorphosis. First it absorbs its own eye. Then its "spine," or notocord. Lastly, it eats its own brain. It won't need its brain anymore, because it's done moving around. It cements itself to the bottom of the ocean, headfirst, and spends the rest of its life eating.

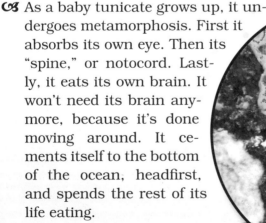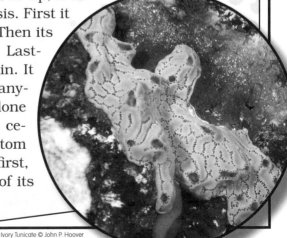

Ivory Tunicate © John P. Hoover

Curious Critters

Hawai'i's creatures come in all shapes, textures and sizes. There are frogs the size of quarters, and toads as big as your hand. Animals with hooves, tusks, antlers, feathers and super-special sticky feet. Do you ever wonder what animals think of us? What goes a gecko think about, for example, as it stares down at us from its perch on the ceiling? Well, one thing is for sure: Mother Nature must have a good sense of humor, because there are some seriously odd things happening in the animal kingdom. Check these out!

Axis Deer

Cute little deer, nibbling innocently on some grass. They couldn't cause any problems, right? Wrong. Axis deer are trying to take over the planet! These deer were first brought to Hawai'i in 1868 as a gift to King Kamehameha V from the governor of Hong Kong. Seemed nice enough, but there's one problem: they multiply. The deer population is booming—there are twenty to thirty percent more of them each year, and they are now found on the Big Island, Maui, O'ahu, Moloka'i and Lāna'i.

The deer move in herds, eating whatever grass and plants they can find. On Maui, for example, they caused two million dollars in damage in just two years. They eat farmers' crops and poop all over the place. They also cause erosion, because they've eaten so many plants.

Axis Deer © H. Douglas Pratt

Fun fact: Male axis deer have more facial markings, giving them the appearance that they are scowling. Males also have antlers, which they grow and shed.

Yikes. In Sri Lanka, where axis deer originally came from, their natural predator is the Bengal tiger. Good thing we don't have any of those roaming around Maui!

Bufo Toad

Big and warty, the Bufo toad was originally brought to Hawai'i to help sugar-cane plantation farmers. The toads' job was supposed to be to eat a pest, the sugar cane beetle. The toads are happy and well-fed in the Islands, and soon, there were a million toads. Literally.

Danger! These big guys—about six inches long—have toxic skin. And, they also give off white toxic goo if they are scared. If a cat or dog licks the toad, they can become very sick or even die from this poison.

Bufo Toad © H. Douglas Pratt

Toad-ally bald? In Japan, the toxic Bufo goo is used as a hair-restorer.

Ten to fifteen years a Bufo toad lives in the wild. A pet toad can live up to thirty-five years.

5 1/2 pounds

That's the weight of the biggest Bufo toad ever found.

Weird fact: The Bufo toads found in Florida are way more toxic than Bufo toads in Hawai'i.

Airlifted Donkeys

The herds of donkeys that used to live on the Big Island, along the road between Kona and Waikoloa, have been gradually disappearing. They are the wild descendants of donkeys used on coffee plantations in the old days. But the herd kept growing, and people were worried that the wandering donkeys would get hit by cars, or might starve if they didn't get enough to eat. So slowly, people in Hawai'i who own farms or have big yards in agricultural areas have adopted the donkeys. Some of the donkeys were even airlifted to California, where they live on an animal sanctuary. It's a happy ending for the donkeys, who are now safe and cared for, whether they live in Hawai'i or not.

Coqui Frog

Small in stature, but hugely annoying, coqui frogs give off a shrieking mating call. It's louder than an alarm clock buzzing or a gas leaf blower—and only slightly quieter than a chainsaw. (A chainsaw gives off a 105 decibels; a coqui frog, ninety-five decibels.) They've pretty much overrun the Big Island, driving people crazy with their nonstop croaking from dusk to dawn.

On O'ahu, they are still trying to keep them from spreading and send out a "frog busting" team to get rid of the frogs before they can spread. The only way the anti-frog team can get rid of the frogs is to spray citric acid, a natural fruit acid. You've eaten it, and lived to tell! Gasp! Well, it's safe for people and used in food to give it a tangy taste, like in sour gummy worms. During a bad invasion, in Wahiawa, in 2001, workers used fire hoses to spray the citric acid all over the place. It took five years of spraying to get rid of the coquis there for good.

© Roy Chang

Coqui frogs are only about the size of a quarter. The females don't make noise but the males sure cause a ruckus.

Clogged up with frogs: On the Big Island, there can be up to ten thousand of these frog pests per acre. Yellow or brown, they can easily blend into the foliage.

Kill them with kindness? Scientists are trying to figure out other ways to kill off the frogs, including spraying them with soap, Tylenol, caffeine, seawater and hot water.

Coqui frogs arrived as stowaways in plants coming in from Puerto Rico, their normal habitat, in the late 1980s.

Geckos Galore!

In Hawai'i, you can find many kinds of geckos: Mourning, Stump-toed, Indopacific, Small Tree, Tokay, Giant Day, Fox, Common House, Orange-Spotted and the fancy sounding Gold-dust Day Gecko. They eat mosquitoes and tackle cockroaches; they're cute; they don't hurt humans. What's not to love? Well, they do poop all over the place. But other than that, we love them. Maybe someone could invent some tiny gecko diapers for inside our houses? Here are 10 amazing gecko facts!

❶ How do geckos go up the wall and not fall off? Millions of tiny hairs on their feet act like stickers or Velcro, helping them defy gravity. Geckos can stick to almost everything—except Teflon, that anti-stick stuff they put in the bottom of pans so the fried eggs will slide off. Wet, dry, smooth or rough, tree or glass... a gecko is comfortable on any surface.

❷ A gecko can hang by just one toe, even from a smooth glass surface.

❸ Their toes bend in the opposite direction that our human toes bend in.

❹ Their footpads are self-cleaning.

❺ After a gecko eats, it cleans its mouth with its tongue.

❻ Geckos also clean their eyeballs using their tongue. Can you do that? They do this because most gecko species don't have eyelids that move.

❼ Geckos are the only lizards that vocalize—they squawk, chirp and click. This is how they talk to each other.

❽ The biggest geckos in the world are twelve inches long; the smallest, only one inch, even when they are fully-grown.

❾ Ewww… Leopard geckos eat their own skin after they shed it. This keeps them on the low-down, so predators aren't aware of them.

❿ They have a sweet tooth. If you want geckos around, feed them honey or jam.

© Roy Chang

A Tale of Tails

If a gecko is being attacked, such as by a bird, it will twist its tail sharply and the tail will fall off. They can do this because the bones in their tails have little cracks so the tail can pop off easily. The muscles and nerves in the tail keep the tail twitching, distracting the bird from eating the whole gecko while it makes its escape. Some types of geckos go a step further and shed their whole skin to escape.

Gold Dust Day Gecko © H. Douglas Pratt

Faking It

Some kinds of geckos rub their scales together, making a sound that imitates a snake to scare off their predators.

Goats Gone Wild

Feral goats © H. Douglas Pratt

Feral goats trample and eat their way through everything. Forests, trees, shrubs, scrubland, grassland, and farm—if it's a green area, they will nosh their way through it. This hurts native species and causes erosion. Some islands in the Pacific have been completely stripped of all plants by wild goats—there's nothing left but dirt. It's called desertification, when a formerly green place becomes desert-like. Still, there are a few interesting things about goats.

➡ Captain Cook released goats in Hawai'i, so this type of animal has been here since about 1778. During that time, sailors routinely put goats on Pacific Islands when they went by, so that when they came back, they would have a handy supply of fresh goat meat.

➡ Wild, or feral goats, like to live up high, at 2,000 to 5,000 feet above sea level. They don't mind if the ground is rough: Lava fields, steep cliffs and rocky canyons are as comfy to a feral goat as your living room is to you.

➡ Goats often give birth to twins.

➡ Both the dude goats and the lady goats have beards.

➡ Their horns are hollow.

➡ Female goats have horns, too, but only male goats butt their horns with each other as a way to display power.

➡ P-U! Males give off a smelly, oily odor.

➡ It's actually easier to digest goat's milk than cow's milk.

➡ To reach a tasty tree or bush, a goat will stand upright on its hind legs.

➡ Herds of up to 200 goats have been seen in Hawai'i.

➡ Their stomachs have four chambers with some funny names: rumen, reticulum, omasum, and the abomasums. Don't you feel smart just saying that?

Attack of the feral chickens

Power to the Poultry

In February 2013, a feral chicken got into an electrical transformer, knocking out power to Kahului Airport on Maui. Security screenings had to be done by hand, rental car companies had no electricity, and planes needed stairs brought to them because the electric jet ways wouldn't work. All this for a…fried chicken.

$200,000

That's how much Maui Mayor Alan Arakawa wants to give to the Humane Society to help deal with Maui's growing feral chicken problem.

feral hen with chicks © H. Douglas Pratt

Poultry on the loose!

Kaua'i has the most feral chickens running around. They're descended from domestic birds that got loose during Hurricane 'Iniki in 1992. Other islands have feral chickens, too, but also have mongooses, which eat the chickens and help keep the population down. On the plus side, chickens dine on centipedes. If you have to choose between being awakened by a rooster crowing and a centipede scurrying across your foot, well, maybe getting up early isn't so bad.

© Roy Chang

Can't we just eat them?

If a chicken wanders onto your property, yes; if it's on public property, no. But you'll need to cook them a long time because their meat is much tougher than that of a chicken you'd buy in the supermarket. Famously un-delicious.

Feral hen © H. Douglas Pratt

1.500 YEARS

That's how long chickens have been in the Islands, brought here by seafaring people from the Marquesas Islands. People from Tahiti brought bigger, more colorful chickens 500 years after that.

Hoary Bat

Swooping in at night, 'ōpe'ape'a, Hawai'i's hoary bat, loves to eat bugs. First off, what does "hoary" mean? Frosted. It's got brownish hair that is gray on the ends. 'Ōpe'ape'a like to dine on termites, crickets, moths and their favorite dish: beetles. They can eat up to forty percent of their body weight at a meal. This animal is solitary—it likes to live alone—and it's endangered, so if you spot one flying above you, consider yourself very lucky.

Hoary Bat © H. Douglas Pratt

Bat Rumor, Debunked

For a while, there was a rumor that bat poo, called guano, is used to make ladies' makeup. But it was a mistake: guano just sounds like a real ingredient in mascara, guanine. And that expression "batting your lashes," just means flirting with someone you think is cute—there's no bat poop involved.

Akepa Hawai'i © H. Douglas Pratt

Just flew in... Scientists think that hoary bats originally got to Hawai'i by being blown in by the wind, from either North or South America.

Mongoose

In 1883, mongooses were brought to Hawai'i to solve a problem—they were supposed to eat the rats on sugar cane plantations. So did they do their job? Did they snack on the rodents? Nope. They eat a few here and there, but rats are active at night and mongooses sleep in their dens at night. The deadly dinner party just didn't happen because they kept missing each other. Then the Islands had rats and mongooses, which reproduce fast.

> Mongeese? No, the plural of mongoose is mongooses.

Surprise, I'm Back!

Three birds that hadn't been seen in decades suddenly appeared in 2012. Scientists had assumed the birds—the akepa, akiapola'au and a type of Hawaiian honeycreeper—were extinct, but then they were suddenly spotted in a national wildlife refuge. Where have you been, guys?

Fun Facts

Some species of Hawaiian honeycreeper have stinky feathers. This is to make them less tasty to predators.

What's On the Menu?

Voracious mongooses like to eat bird eggs, baby birds, and turtles—including some endangered species. To open an egg, a mongoose will throw it with its front paws onto a solid object, cracking it open. Slugs, spiders, snails, frogs, crabs, fish, plants, chicken, ducks, fruit and small mammals (lock up your kittens!) are also considered tasty by a mongoose, as are dead animals—that's called carrion. Fierce fighters, mongooses usually kill their prey by biting the back of the other animal's head. In places where they have snakes, mongooses are famous for eating venomous types, like cobras.

Mongoose © H. Douglas Pratt

Ewww!

Their droppings can spread a disease called leptospirosis, which can make people sick.

Mongooses in History

A 1911 article in *The Hawaiian Star* tells us how mongooses steal eggs from henhouses: They spit in the face of the hen, then grab the egg and run.

Shameless Rumor

Supposedly, there was a hotel on the Big Island that ran a special: If you ran over a mongoose with your car, you'd get a free night's stay there. To prove you killed it, your car's tire treads had to match the tread marks on the dead mongoose.

Mongoose in ANCIENT History:

According to National Geographic, mummified mongooses have been found in Egyptian tombs.

Mynah Birds

Strutting around like tough little body builders, mynah birds act like they rule the roost. Which they do. This type of bird was brought to Hawai'i in 1865, to eat other pests: cutworms and armyworms. But there are so many mynah birds, now they are considered the pests.

Most people in Hawai'i hate mynahs, though the birds are quite smart, because they make an awful lot of noise, spread diseases like salmonella, and they eat trash. The Hawaiian words for them are piha'ekelo (full of voice) and manu'aipilau (trash-eating bird). But in some parts of the world, they are cherished pets. **Did you know...**

🪶 They are brilliant mimics who can fake human speech—or even the sound of a bicycle. A mynah can learn up to about one hundred words.

🪶 Trash! Delish! It's one of their favorite foods, which alas, means they often have liver problems. They also like to eat insects.

🪶 Very aggressive and territorial, mynahs will attack other birds, even occasionally, humans. (I once tried to shoo a mynah bird away with a broom and it was not scared of me at all. I was scared of it!)

🪶 In Sanskrit, the word for this kind of bird is kalahapriya, or "one who is fond of arguments," because they squawk so loudly.

🪶 Whoops... One of the problems with invasive birds is that people slip on their droppings.

🪶 Mynahs are usually found in pairs.

MYNOKEA

© Roy Chang

Unwelcome Visitors

Hawai'i has such special and unusual animals and plants; it would be devastating to bring in new animals that will disturb the balance. For example, Hawai'i doesn't have the disease rabies here, but other states in the U.S. do. It would be terrible if it came to the Islands. Or snakes; if they arrived, they would start eating all the birds. So when people bring in animals that don't belong here, the authorities have to take them away. Here are some of the animals that have been discovered and removed:

❶ **Albino snake.** It was found when it was accidentally weed-whacked to death by a landscaping crew near the Honolulu International Airport.

❷ **Boa constrictor.** A six-foot-long snake was captured in a garage on the Big Island.

❸ **Burmese python.** When it was loose near Makawao on Maui, state officials went on a massive hunt using shotguns, rifles, handguns and machetes.

❹ **Bearded dragon lizard.**

❺ **Live bat.** The man who brought it in illegally was playing with it, tossing it in the air near Baggage Claim B of the Honolulu International Airport. Which is dumber: smuggling in a bat, or playing with a smuggled bat?

❻ **Ferret.** It escaped from a motor scooter and was captured in a parking lot in Hilo.

❼ **Corn snake.**

❽ **Sugar glider.** That's a small, Australian possum-like critter some people like as pets.

Deportation Section

© Roy Chang

These animals are illegal in Hawai'i, too: Wolf-dog crossbreeds, dingoes, wild hares, wild mustangs, lemmings, and snapping turtles. Gerbils and hamsters are far more ordinary pets, but they aren't allowed either.

I've Got a Bite

In 1993, a fisherman at the Wahiawa Reservoir caught a piranha on O'ahu! It was the second one caught within an eight-month period. They were frozen and examined by scientists. The fish probably got there when someone who was keeping them illegally as pets released them. Luckily, no more piranhas have been seen.

Holy Smoke!

When firefighters went to a 2011 fire in 'Ālewa Heights, on O'ahu, they found more than smoke and flames. They also discovered a five-foot-long boa constrictor and four piranhas.

$200,000

That's the fine you have to pay if you're found to be keeping an lady animal in your house. You might have to serve up to three years in jail, too.

Monk Seal

The Hawaiian name for monk seal, 'ilio holo i ka uaua, means "dog running in the rough water" and another name, na mea hulu, means "the furry one." This animal is endemic to Hawai'i; that means it wasn't brought here by humans and can't be seen any other place on Earth. Seals have been in Hawai'i a long time: several million years.

Diving deep. To chase its food—an octopus, eel or crab—a monk seal can dive down 1,500 feet. That's about as long as the Empire State Building is tall! Their bodies have a cool trick: the heart rate slows down while they are diving, so they don't need as much oxygen and can stay under the water longer. On the surface of the water, their heart beats eight times faster than it does when they are diving.

© Rohichs | Dreamstime.com

These extremely endangered animals are the only marine mammal found just in waters around the United States. It's also Hawai'i's official state mammal.

Growing fast. A baby monk seal, or pup, is born on land. They only weigh thirty pounds or so, but pack on 175 pounds in just a few weeks. Once they are grown ups, they will tip the scales at 400 to 600 pounds and stretch out to about seven feet long.

Do you like to eat lobster? So do monk seals! They also like to eat fish and shrimp, just like you. But they can eat ten percent of their body weight in one day! That's a big appetite.

They need our help. There are only about 1,100 monk seals left. Why? Sharks eat them, and sometimes they attack each other, too, but the main threat to them is humans. We accidentally catch them in fishing nets; leave marine trash that hurts them; and have changed their shoreline habitat.

Camping out. During a storm, a monk seal will come onto shore and hide under the bushes near the ocean.

ZZZZZZ...

Napping on the beach is a favorite pastime; this is called "hauling out." But sometimes, seals snooze underwater. Scuba divers can see monk seals taking a nap underwater in a sea cave. How cool is that? A group of monk seals is called a "colony or rookery." But they are usually very solitary— that means they like to be alone.

zzzzz zzzzz

© Roy Chang

Bite you in the butt?

Not usually! A tourist was bitten in the buttock when he got too close to a monk seal in the water off Po'ipū on Kaua'i. He didn't need stitches, but he had to get a tetanus shot. And new swimming trunks.

Hair, begone.

About once a year, a monk seal sheds its top layer of skin and fur. If you see a monk seal that is kind of greenish, it means it has algae growing on it and hasn't shed in a while. It's probably getting ready to molt, or take off that top layer, soon. Do you think you would grow algae on you if you didn't take a bath? Hmm.

Nēnē

Our state bird has an interesting history. Nēnē were almost wiped out by the 1940s; people had been allowed to hunt and eat them until 1907; dogs, cats and mongooses had also lowered their numbers. Nēnē nearly became extinct and there were only about thirty of them left. Luckily they have been making a comeback and can again be seen in the wild.

© Steven Oehlenschlager | Dreamstime.com

◆ Unlike other geese, nēnē have only part-webbed feet.

◆ And unlike most geese, they don't migrate, or fly anywhere when the seasons change.

◆ Their feet are part clawed, to help them walk on lava.

◆ Nēnē eggs look a lot like chicken eggs, but a little smaller.

◆ It's illegal to touch or bother one of these birds, but because they aren't scared of humans, they might come right up to you. They are very curious about what you are doing.

◆ Think they look like Canadian geese? They were, when the birds arrived in the Islands a half a million years ago. Over time, they adapted and changed, becoming the unique nēnē bird.

◆ What do you call a whole bunch of geese? You can call them a knot, a plump, a blizzart or a string of geese.

Poi Dogs

Nowadays, the term "poi dog" has come to mean a mixed-breed dog, or even an easygoing, non-snooty mixed dog. Your family might have one of those "lab-chow-we think part collie" kine, for example. But did you know that there used to be a special breed of dog in Hawai'i, also called a poi dog, that has now gone extinct?

Weird science: Supposedly, in 1967, the Honolulu Zoo's director, Jack Thorpe, headed a breeding program to see if the extinct poi dog could be recreated, but the experiment failed.

© Dennis Crow | Dreamstime.com

© Erik Lam | Dreamstime.com

Rambo

People in 'Aiea were very surprised to see a ram wandering through their backyards, hopping over fences and enjoying the neighborhood. The strange 2011 sighting of this mixed-breed sheep with big, curling horns had everyone talking. Soon, the mystery was solved: Rambo was an illegal pet who lived in Pearl City. When the state officials came to take Rambo, the ram's owner shot him. Right in front of the officials! How crazy is that? He said he would rather eat him than let him be taken away.

Rats

Hawai'i has three kinds of rats—but the Best Name Award goes to Rattus Rattus, also known as the roof rat or the black rat. It's a great climber, and loves to go up into trees. It can even walk across a telephone or power line. Roof rats love to eat fruit (their favorite is oranges), avocadoes, and macadamia nuts. Up to ten percent of each year's mac-nut crop gets enjoyed by rats, instead of us humans. The other two rat species you can find in the Islands are the Polynesian and the Norway rat. Here are some rat tails...uh, I mean, tales. ➔

© Roy Chang

Black Roof Rat © H. Douglas Pratt

R a t s are really good swimmers. They can swim up to a mile, and can tread water for three days.

Wiggle, wiggle. The jaw muscle on a rat runs under its eye socket, beneath the eyeball, so when a rat is chewing hard, his eyes will "boggle," or move in and out. That sounds alarming!

Superhero rat? A rat can fall from a fifty-foot height and live to tell. They can chew through aluminum, cinder block, even lead. And they can squeeze their whole body into your house through a hole that's the size of a quarter.

Call the dentist! Rats only have one set of teeth—and they are a nasty yellow color—that grow and grow through their lives, at a rate of four inches a year. If the rat's teeth get out of alignment, they will start to curl back as they grow, piercing through the top of their mouths.

Rattail
A hairstyle popular in the 1980s. Hair is shorter on top but has a skinny, long "tail" in the back.

Gonna need a lot of toilet paper.
A single rat will poop 40 to 50 times in one day.

There's a rat killer in Hawaiian mythology. Pōkoi was such an excellent rat hunter that he once killed 40 at once, striking them through with an arrow. He also shot so well, he could pierce the whiskers of a rat. In another Hawaiian myth, the 'Ioleka'a Valley on O'ahu had vicious rats who would lure other rats to their deaths. They'd lure them to a slippery stone on a cliff, and then they'd lose their footing and fall into the stream below.

© Maksym Bondarchuk | Dreamstime.com

Roof Rat © H. Douglas Pratt

Wallabies

More cute than creepy, wallabies are still interesting. Yes, O'ahu is home to brush-tailed rock wallabies. What's a wallaby, you might ask. A small kangaroo, basically, about knee-high and up to 18 pounds. They are brown, with reddish fur on their rear ends and long, bushy tails. They are the relatives of a pair of wallabies who escaped from a private zoo in 1916. You might see one in Kalihi Valley, but they are hard to spot and no one knows how many live there. They are shy and like to eat Christmas berry bushes.

© Andygwior | Dreamstime.com

Wild Pigs

Big, beady-eyed eating machines, Hawai'i's feral pigs are a mix, a blend of the pigs Polynesians brought to the Islands for food, and the wild Eurasian boar, and domestic "farm" pigs.

Young feral pigs © H. Douglas Pratt

Quit hogging our stuff!

Feral pigs are a far more than just a nuisance.

❶ They trample over plants, and spread weeds from one area to another.

❷ Pigs dig with their snouts; this kills a plant all the way down to its roots so that it can't ever recover.

❸ They wallow in wet forests, scooping out pits to take a bath in. Those water-filled holes become a breeding ground for mosquitoes. Mosquitoes spread Avian flu to the birds.

❹ Pigs even destroy the coral reefs. They strip plants from the higher ground, then erosion happens, and all this mud cascades down into the ocean.

❺ Hog poop can get into our drinking water supply and make humans sick.

❻ They only kill five to seven people a year in the U.S., so the risk of being attacked is low, but they do sometimes charge at people, slashing upward with their razor-sharp tusks.

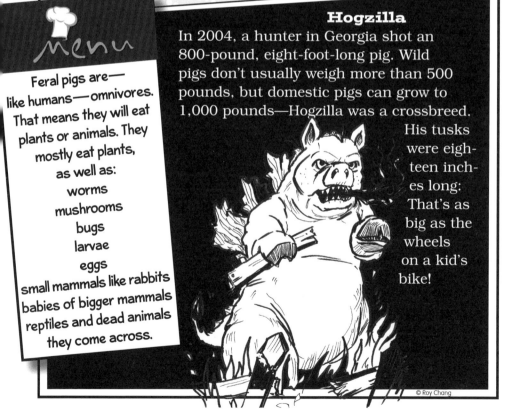

Menu

Feral pigs are—like humans—omnivores. That means they will eat plants or animals. They mostly eat plants, as well as:

worms
mushrooms
bugs
larvae
eggs
small mammals like rabbits
babies of bigger mammals
reptiles and dead animals they come across.

Hogzilla

In 2004, a hunter in Georgia shot an 800-pound, eight-foot-long pig. Wild pigs don't usually weigh more than 500 pounds, but domestic pigs can grow to 1,000 pounds—Hogzilla was a crossbreed. His tusks were eighteen inches long: That's as big as the wheels on a kid's bike!

© Roy Chang

Revenge of the Humans

Hunting pigs is legal in Hawai'i and many people like to eat the meat. Wild boar can be smoked, made into lau lau or kālua pig, served as ham or made into sausage. If you're still hungry, there's boar served in stew, adobo, or ragu sauce, as pork loin, on skewers and in corn dogs. Don't forget boar bacon! In England, a traditional Christmas feast used to include a boar's head served on a platter. Eating well is the best revenge.

Did You Know?

Pigs have amazing senses of smell. They can smell something that is five to seven miles away from them, and can even smell food that's buried twenty-five feet underground. That's why pig hunters use special "descenting" soap before a hunt, so they'll be able to sneak up on the hog. Serious hunters avoid eating spicy or strong foods, like red meat, hot sauce, onions and garlic, and wash their clothes in baking soda, or special detergents, instead of regular soap, so the pigs won't smell them coming. Special "rotting meat" incense can be used to get clothes to smell … well, less human. But what if a hunter has to pee? Here's the gross solution: They use a hunter's pouch, which hides the pee scent with a scentless gel.

How fast do you think a feral pig could run?

Pigs are all grunty and porky, so you might think they can only waddle slowly. Actually, they can go up to thirty miles an hour, and they can jump over a three-foot-high fence.

Young feral pig © H. Douglas Pratt

The Supernatural

Does your dog ever bark for no reason? Or maybe the hair on the back of your neck sticks up, and you get the feeling you are being watched? Maybe you are. The Islands are full of ghost stories, and, since almost everything is built over an ancient burial ground, it's easy to become a true believer in otherworldly visitors. Native Hawaiian stories tell of rascal spirits, elves, and the fearsome Night Marchers. Other cultures, from places like Thailand and the Philippines, brought their own scary tales with them when they came to Hawai'i. The resulting mix is a spicy melting pot of Hawai'i's spooky legends and folklore. So if you love to get chicken-skin, read on. (Whether you leave the night light on or not is up to you.)

Bundle Keepers

People are not always what they seem. Some of your so-called friends or family members could secretly be a he mālama pū'olo, or bundle keeper. This is a person who steals things—a lock of hair, nail clippings, or even excrement—in order to control someone else, or, to put a curse onto them. If this evil-doer can't get a hunk of you, he will switch to another tactic: sending you a present. Be on the lookout for someone who suddenly gives you a lei or a gift for no reason at all.

Dog-Man

A supernatural dog-man once ruled Nu'uanu Valley. His name was Kaupe, and to give you a sense of his sparkling personality, the same Hawaiian word also means "to crush." Kaupe could appear as a dog or a man, AND he was also a cannibal. He ate many of the people of O'ahu. Once he'd gotten his fill, or maybe he'd just eaten all the tastiest citizens, he flew to Maui and then to the Big Island in search of more people to eat. He was eventually killed, but his ghost lives on and can still be seen in the dark clouds that gather in the highest parts of Nu'uanu Valley.

Egghead Ghost

A couple in 'Ewa Beach awoke one night to the sound of tapping, writes Glen Grant in *Glen Grant's Chicken Skin Tales: 49 Favorite Ghost Stories from Hawai'i*. It kind of sounded like geta, old-fashioned, Japanese wooden sandals, clomping down the sidewalk. But who would be wearing geta in this day and age, and in the middle of the night? So the husband got out of bed to investigate and looked out the window. He saw an elderly Japanese woman, wearing a kimono and geta, and holding a red parasol. Thinking she was cute, he called to his wife to come see. The wife looked down, too, and as the old Japanese woman passed the window, she lowered her parasol, as if she were about to wave hello. But the couple was stunned by what they saw. "Both of their knees buckled as their flesh tingled," Grant says. Because the woman had no eyes, no mouth, and no nose. She was as featureless and smooth as a white egg.

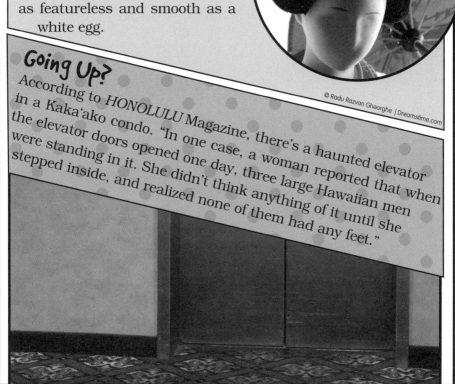

© Radu Razvan Gheorghe | Dreamstime.com

Going Up?

According to *HONOLULU* Magazine, there's a haunted elevator in a Kaka'ako condo. "In one case, a woman reported that when the elevator doors opened one day, three large Hawaiian men were standing in it. She didn't think anything of it until she stepped inside, and realized none of them had any feet."

Meet the Hawaiian Phantoms

Akualele: Fireballs, which are the spirits of a deceased person. They've frequently been reported near Ka'ena Point, where spirits leap from this world into the next.

Akua hele loa: Trouble-making ghosts. They are sent forth by sorcerers to destroy other people.

'E'epas: Hawaiian gnomes. Deformed, they are twisted in both mind and body. They are treacherous and will some-times appear as a human, though that human will also have a deformity. Occasionally, they are kinder hearted and will take care of children.

Kolohe: Mischievous, rascal spirits.

Kupua: Demigods who can magically change form, or who appear in two different forms. Take Kamapua'a, for ex-ample. He could be a handsome man, tall with sparkling eyes. But under his cape, he's hiding the bristles that run down his back. Because he is also a brutal, grunting hog.

Lapu: A wandering soul.

Menehune: Strong, sturdy dwarves, these expert stone-masons could build a whole fishpond or ditch in one night.

Mo'o: Dragon-like reptiles, like giant lizards. For example, one lives under Mo'oula Falls on Moloka'i. Swimmers should drop a ti leaf into the pool there if they want to swim. If the leaf floats, it's safe to go in, but if it sinks, the mo'o is not in the mood for company.

'Unihipili: A ghost used to do the evil work of a sorcerer.

Half-Faced Ghost

A half-faced specter is seen along the Old Pali Road on O'ahu. She's the ghost of a girl, a freshman in high school, who was strangled with a jump rope and left in the bushes. Now she comes skipping out of the afterlife and down the road at you, long black hair floating behind her. Her eyes bulge out of her face, since she was strangled, but much of her face is miss-ing. She has no cheeks, nose or mouth.

Ghosts in the John

✤ Japanese ghosts seem to like bathrooms. You've got the ghost in the outhouse, which wafts bits of poop onto people it doesn't like.

✤ Inside bathrooms are the domain of the akaname, which loves dirty tubs. It feeds on the icky blobs of mildew around the edges—wait, if this ghost is scrubbing the tub with its tongue, isn't that kind of a help? Thanks, akaname!

✤ The akamanto sounds downright scary. While you're sitting on the toilet, you'll hear a voice asking you if you would like a red cape. If you say yes, it will rip the skin right off your back.

✤ The "ceiling licker," or tenjōname, can be found hovering mid-air. It uses its super-long tongue to lick the ceiling, leaving strange stains and blobs up there.

A Tongan ghost called a Fehuluni takes her head off her shoulders and puts it in her lap so that she can comb her hair.

© Roy Chang

© Roy Chang

In Filipino culture, an amamanhig is a deceased person who can't lie down in their coffin. They keep getting up to take care of something, but they can't remember what. And since they can't think on their own anymore, they just repeat the words of everyone around them. Sounds like a horrible party guest!

Haunted Schools

Lahainaluna High School on Maui has been called a hot spot for spirits, with mysterious shadows moving around. Supposedly, a ghost of a dog roams the halls at night, followed by the misty apparition of the man who owned the dog.

Students in **The University of Hawai'i-Mānoa's** Mokihana Hale dormitory have reported strange happenings. For example, the sense that someone is whispering in their ear at night, or small paper juice cups mysteriously appearing. Hamilton Library has apparitions hanging out in the library stacks.

La Pietra has strange breezes, and many people who walk the grounds there say they have felt the presence of something—or someone—including a guardian-type male.

According to the student news *Chaminade Silversword*, **Chaminade University** "is haunted all over the place." It reported, "Not only have residents at both Keiffer and Lokelani reported multiple ghost sightings, but also security guards have described experiencing "very strange" activity. "I have heard a lot of stories from all of my coworkers," former Chaminade security officer Jaman said during an interview with Anthony Dujmovic. "One time in Eiben Hall we were in there locking up the building and our radio walkies shut off and no one could radio anyone or anything. When we walked outside the doors shut automatically behind us and then the walkies suddenly came back on. It was very scary."

Don't whistle after dark. It attracts ghosts.

How to Revive the Dead

Kāpuku means "restoring the dead to life," and "kilokilo 'uhane" is a ritual used to raise the dead. This theme comes up in many Hawaiian stories. Let's see how the process works, in the legend of Eleio, recorded by Johannes C. Andersen.

"The spirit of the girl had been lingering near him all the time, seeming to be attracted to him, but of course invisible to everyone else. When he had finished his invocation, he turned and caught the spirit, and holding his breath and invoking the gods, he hurried to the pūʻoʻa [a lean-to for depositing a corpse in] ... he placed the spirit against the insteps of the girl and pressed it firmly in, meanwhile continuing his invocation. The spirit entered its former body kindly enough until it came to the knees, when it refused to go further, fearing pollution, but Eleio by the strength of his prayers induced it to go farther, and farther, the father and mother, and male relatives assisting with their prayers, and at length, the spirit was persuaded to take entire possession of the body, and the girl came to life again."

Images at the Mausoleum

Mauna ʻAla, the royal mausoleum on Nuʻuanu Avenue in Honolulu, is the perpetual home of Hawaiʻi's rulers. There lies the ʻiwi of all the Kamehamehas except Kamehameha the Great, whose remains were hidden and remain so. When four-year-old Prince Albert died, he, too, was buried there in August 1862. It's also the final resting spot for Charles Reed Bishop, who built the Kamehameha crypt.

All that energy, that mana, leads to some seriously weird things happening with cameras. For example, when a crew came to film at Mauna ʻAla for a local TV show, the tape rolled, but recorded absolutely nothing. The viewfinder wouldn't work, either. Once the crew asked the spirits for their blessing, though, the tape and viewfinder started working again perfectly.

There's also a famous image of the ghostly image of Charles Reed Bishop in the window of the Kamehameha crypt, where his wife and her relatives are buried. An art student had taken a photo of the building, and when he developed the film, he discovered a man's face, with a beard and glasses, seemingly at the window.

Mauna Ala © Douglas Peebles

Night Marchers

Ka Huaka I a ka Po, the Marchers of the Night, are the spirits of dead chiefs and chieftesses, warriors and priests, and their attendants. They come on Akua, the fourteenth, or Kāne, the twenty-seventh, night of the lunar cycle, usually between 7:30 p.m. and 2 a.m. Seven feet tall, the Night Marchers float above the ground, but strangely, still can leave footprints. The warriors are dressed in malos, with short, feathered capes, and carry spears.

People who have encountered the Night Marchers tell of hearing the sound of drums and chanting. Tree branches snap and a smell—musky, foul—fills the air. There's the call of a conch shell, and someone yelling "Kapu moe!", telling them to

How to Revive the Dead 2

In *Hawaiian Legends of Volcanoes*, author William Westervelt shares this similar story, about Pele's sister, Hi'iaka, helping the family of a man who had drowned while fishing.

"Hi'iaka slapped the ghost back against the body and told it to go in at the bottom of the feet. She slapped the feet again and again, but it was very hard to push the ghost inside. It tried to come out as fast as Hi'iaka pushed it in. Then Hi'iaka uttered an incantation, while she struck the feet and limbs. Hi'iaka had forced the ghost up to the hips. There was a hard struggle and ancient chants for the restoration of life. All this time she was slapping and pounding the spirit into the body. It had gone up as far as the chest. Then she took fresh water and poured it over the eyes, dashing it into the face. The ghost leaped up to the mouth and eyes— choking noises were made—the eyes opened faintly and closed again, but the ghost was entirely in the body. Slowly life returned. ...

The fisherman had been brought back to life."

© Roy Chang

get down on the ground. In the distance, they see a red glow or red lights—the torches of the marchers. There are well-known paths for the Night Marchers, who are often seen near the ruins of heiau or on the sites of ancient battles, always heading from mauka to makai. And they don't stop; night marchers pass right through a stone wall or into a river, or in and out of buildings and houses. They've been spotted in:

- ❀ Upcountry Moloka'i, near Maunaloa, and in the town of Kaunakakai, near the Ili'ili'opae heiau. Built in the thirteenth century, that heiau was known as a school for sorcerers and the site of many human sacrifices.
- ❀ Waipi'o Valley on the Big Island.
- ❀ La Pérouse Bay, in South Maui, where they roam

along the hardened lava ground.

* Moanalua Valley, running through Kaiser Hospital. At Kaiser, by the way, when someone dies, they open a window so that the soul can get out.
* The Kamehameha Schools campus in Kapalama, where they roam halls and knock on doors.
* Near Merchant and Alakea in Honolulu, where they supposedly laugh and play games in the street.
* The "S" turn in Waipahu, near the Kīpapa Valley Gulch. Kīpapa Gulch was once the site of a huge battle.
* National Memorial Cemetery of the Pacific, inside Punchbowl.
* Near the trail head of the hike to Mānoa Falls.

If you're lucky, your 'aumakua will claim you for the living and push you to the ground before you look at the Night Marchers directly: that would lead to certain death. But if you don't have an 'aumakua, quickly lay down on your stomach and look away!

Lava = Bad Luck?

Many years ago, a ranger at Hawai'i Volcanoes National Park, Russ Apple, was getting tired of watching visitors to the park taking rocks home with them. So he made up a story that Pele would curse anyone who took a lava rock. The myth stuck, and now, each year, people mail lava and black sand to hotels, the park and places like Volcano Gallery on the Big Island, which has a service that helps people return them to Madam Pele. The visitors are convinced that since they look the lava, they have had massive problems. In their letters to Volcano Gallery, they blame the rocks for causing:

* Cancer
* Hospitalizations
* Lawn tractor accident
* Getting laid off from a job
* Death in the family

* Foreclosure on home
* Hurt shoulder while working out
* Had to put the cat to sleep
* Depression
* Broke up with girlfriend

- Television conked out
- Lost wedding ring
- Total blindness
- Rock landed on windshield
- Car accidents
- Mother-in-law broke arm
- Dog jumped through window and had to get $423 worth of stitches
- Had to put grandmother in a nursing home

- Dog got sprayed by a skunk
- New computer stopped working
- Divorce and separations
- Five-week long cold
- Huge medical bills
- Vacant rental house
- Lost luggage
- Early labor
- A robbery
- Having to replace the brakes on the car
- Lost financial aid to college
- Brain tumor

Jeez, superstition or not, I wouldn't risk taking any lava, anywhere!

Military Ghosts

Schofield Barracks has ghosts who will tug at blankets and horse around, laughing.

- ✓ Objects move around and stack themselves on Ford Island, and appliances will suddenly turn on and off.
- ✓ A partially transparent man dressed in a World War II soldier's uniform has been seen at the water's edge of Alanahihi Point, on the Big Island.
- ✓ Hickam Air Force Base has a ghost named Charley who likes to change the station on radios. One hundred eighty-nine men died there during the attack on Pearl Harbor.

The Haunted Collector Visits Hawai'i

The Unhappy Maid

You wouldn't expect the president of Castle & Cooke Resorts to be a believer in ghosts, but even bigwigs can experience a haunting. Its president, a man named Steve Bumbar, invited the SyFy program "Haunted Collector," to come to Lāna'i to investigate, because strange things were happening in some of the company's buildings. For example, Mr. Bumbar had been sleeping in a former carriage house, which is now a guesthouse, when the bed started violently shaking. It was 3:30 a.m. It finally stopped, but he found he couldn't move. "My eyes could open but I couldn't scream," he said on the show. "I couldn't say anything. I was frozen."

Meanwhile, over in the Social Hall, one witness reported that every single window had opened and closed, at 2 a.m. These are heavy windows. And this went on for twenty minutes.

The "Haunted Collector" crew went to work to find out what was causing these occurrences. Did the iculanibokola they found have anything to do with it? Maybe. That's a wooden fork from Fiji, where it was used by cannibals to eat their enemies and take their souls. No; the researchers decided it was just a decoration; nothing related to the haunting. Was it the Night Marchers causing the entire ruckus? No, the Social Hall is not in the path of the marchers, according to a local expert the show talked to. But ah ha! The investigators found an underground room and in it was a rusty old bed frame, with a ti leaf wrapped around it. It turned out that a servant on the plantation had killed herself near the Social Hall. The Haunted Collector team removed the bed frame and there have been no more disturbances since.

Meanwhile, over on Maui...

The Haunted Collectors also checked out The 'Iao Theater, built in 1928. The manager there, Michael Pulliam, told them lights go on and off, things come flying off the shelves.

Several people have seen a misty, glowing female. It scares the actors, he says. "You get an overwhelming, 'get out of the building!' feeling, literally shutting down productions." In the dressing rooms, people hear voices, but when they go in, there's no one there.

The investigators found a pāhoa, a dagger that Hawaiian warriors would use in battle. But it was new, not old—just a prop for a play. After digging up a time capsule at the theater, they found an old film reel inside. They got a projector and played it, finding spooky, silent images of a woman. Is it a screen test? Or the woman who haunts the theater? No one is sure yet.

The investigators also set up cameras, and caught images of a white figure on the stage. When they showed it to Michael, he didn't seem scared at all. It was the same ghost he's seen in the theater before. "I'm so pleased and blown away that they were able to capture a piece of video that amazing." A little ghost memorial has been set up for this person, this "Unknown Actress," because they think the spirit wants recognition. "Despite placing the memorial, sightings of the female spirit continue," the show reports.

'Iao Theater © Douglas Peebles

Revenge of the Jilted Bride

© Roy Chang

During Bon Dance Season, you might hear some good Japanese ghost stories, obake stories. Here's a famous one you can scare your friends with:

Once there was a sweet, pretty young woman named Oiwasan, who lived long ago in Tokyo, back when it was still called Edo. She was happily married to a handsome samurai. At least, she thought she was happily married. Her samurai husband had started an affair with the daughter of a wealthy merchant family; he wanted to get rid of Oiwasan and marry the rich girl, instead. So one night, he slipped poison into Oiwasan's dinner. The horrible poison ate through the right side of her face, dissolving her jaw and skin, and she soon died a painful death. The samurai threw his dead wife's body down a well to hide it, and quickly married his new love, the wealthy woman.

Oiwasan's spirit started haunting the house, moaning in pain. Finally, one night, the samurai had had enough of the sound. He leaped up, grabbed his sword and rushed toward the ghost with her disfigured face. Raising his sword, he hacked at the ghost and when she fell down, he rolled her over. To his horror, he found the dead body of his new wife. Oiwasan had tricked him! She got her revenge, but never found peace and still roams through Tokyo at night. Her long, thick hair hides her scarred face, but when someone comes closer, she'll pull it back, revealing her horrible appearance, then disappear laughing when they scream in horror.

The mythical creature most likely to become a cool band name: Supernatural Chicken. (In Hawaiian, that's Ka'auhelemoa.)

The Woman in the Red Dress

A beautiful woman was found wandering the halls of the Hilton Hawaiian Village. When a staff person tried to help her back to her room, she suddenly disappeared. She's been seen by housecleaning staff, and guests, too, and even sighted down on the beach in front of the hotel. If you hear a knock on your door in the middle of the night, it's probably the same mysterious woman in red. Some think she is Madam Pele.

For two centuries, there have been reports of Pele, all over the Islands, often seen as a gorgeous woman wearing a red dress or mu'umu'u. Other times she will appear as a white dog, which means there's about to be a death in the family, or an old, withered woman. She might ask you for a glass of cool water, a chicken, or a ride in your car. Whatever she wants, you should give it to her!

The Dried Fish Ghost

There once was an old man, who left his village and climbed over the summit of Mount Halemanu, on Kaua'i. He got a big bale of dried fish, lugged them over his shoulder and started back on the path, intending to bring all the fish home to his village. But he never arrived. After a few days, people got worried and went looking for him.

They found the old man dead on the mountain path, his head bashed in. Someone had killed him and stolen all his dried fish! His sad friends buried him where they'd found him, near the side of the path. Every year, on the anniversary of his death, his ghost appears in the same spot. You'll know him if you see him—he's the ghost wearing a bundle of dried fish on his back. But I hope you don't run into him; he's waiting to kill the first person who passes by so he can get revenge.

Are you watching the movie, or the ghost at Dole Cannery? The ghost of a man in his mid-fifties will sit down next to you in theater 14.

Thai culture has a creature called a phi kong koi, which lives in the jungle and sucks blood out of the toes of people who come through the forest. It only has one arm and one leg. Another jungle dweller, the phi poang kang, looks more like a monkey and likes to live near a salt lick.

The Lady in White

There's a rumor that if you're driving on an old road in Waipahu, near what was once the O'ahu Sugar Plantation, something terrifying will happen. You'll hit something with your car—at least, you'll feel like you did. When you look back, you'll see the body of a woman in white, crumpled on the road. Then an elderly Filipino lady will stand up and start laughing at you. She's the ghost of a woman who was hit by a truck on the plantation nearly a century ago.

A similar story appears in *Glen Grant's Chicken Skin Tales,* about a woman who had thought she hit a pedestrian one night along the Kamehameha Highway in Kuhuku. Shocked to have hit someone, the driver immediately put the brakes on. "There on the hood of the moving vehicle was a young Hawaiian woman wearing a long, green flowing dress. The look on her face was one of horror and disbelief. Just as the car came to a stop, the girl on the hood lifted her head up on her elbow, peered right in at the driver and changed her expression. A slight kolohe or rascal smile replaced the horror as she gave the driver a malicious wink." Then the ghost stood up on the hood of the car, and jumped straight up, disappearing into the night sky.

Another haunted hotel: At the Waikīkī Parc, a deceased employee still occasionally punches in—though never out—on the work time clock.

An annual Miss Vampire Beauty Pageant is held in Honolulu, in October at the Hawai'i Theatre. It's "like traditional beauty pageants but with a darker twist," the show's promoters say. These bewitching beauties don't compete in a swimsuit category—that would be too sunny! Instead, there's a category called "moonbathing."

© Roy Chang

Thinking to Death

If you believe you've been cursed, will you die? Maybe, according to this report, from Capt. George Anson, who came across a group of Hawaiian men doing magic in 1825.

> "I witnessed, for the first time, a rite of sorcery. A small mat was spread on the ground, on which was spread several pieces of tapa, a native cloth, and on those again two of the large leaves of the ape [plant]…"

When he asked the men there what was going on, they told him that a pipe had been stolen from one of the men, and the incantation was to discover the thief, and to kill him using their chants.

> "Perhaps there is no superstition more general and deep-rooted in the minds of this people than the belief that some have the power of destroying the lives of others by their incantations and prayers. There is not a doubt that many yearly become victims [to their belief] in this device of darkness."

A person is told that the kahuna 'anā'anā (a person trained in sorcery) is exercising his power over him and that he will die. This belief triggers a terrible chain of events.

> "He cannot shake the dread of that which he believes to be possible; his imagination becomes filled with pictures of his death. His appetite fails. He takes no nourishment, pines, languishes and dies, the victim of his own ignorance and superstition. This is no fiction, but a reality that is constantly occurring."

Tofu Ghost

An apparition that looks like a small boy in a kimono, the tofu kozo tries to get mortals to taste his tofu. He'll follow you down the street, wearing an enormous hat made from bamboo. If his tofu has a maple leaf stamped on it, you'll know it's him for sure. Don't eat that tofu! If you do, fungus will start growing through your body from the inside out, causing you agony and finally killing you.

© Roy Chang

Who You Gonna Call?

Spooky Kine Investigations and Hawaiian Island Paranormal Research Societies are both nonprofit paranormal research and investigation groups. They look for evidence of ghosts with electromagnetic frequency detectors, thermometers and night vision cameras.

Word to the Wise

During the twilight time of Obon Season, when the dead can mingle with the living, stay far away from ponds and rivers. Disembodied spirits who don't have any relatives praying for them will lurk near the water, waiting to drag you in and drown you.

The "hopping ghost" is popular in Hong Kong cinema. It's a bloodthirsty corpse who has been dead so long, it can barely move. They have long, blue fingernails. They attack people at the throat but can be scared off by sticky rice.

© Stephen Bures | Dreamstime.com

Visiting the Other Side

What would it be like to die? Everyone has different ideas of what happens. Here's one version by a woman in Kona. It was recorded in 1907's *Thrum's Hawaiian Folk Tales*.

"I died, as you know. I seemed to leave my body and stand beside it, looking down on what was me. The me that was standing there looked like the form I was looking at, only, I was alive and the other was dead. I gazed at my body for a few minutes, then turned and walked away."

She walked through three villages, she said, with hundreds of houses and thousands of men, women, and children.

"Some of them I knew and they spoke to me,—although that seemed strange, for I knew they were dead,—but nearly all were strangers. They were all so happy! They seemed not to have a care; nothing to trouble them. Joy was in every face, and happy laughter and bright, loving words were on every tongue. … I felt so full of joy, too, that my heart sang within me, and I was glad to be dead."

Then she reached the volcano, and was told it was not her time to die.

"They said, 'You must go back to your body. You are not to die yet.'

"I did not want to go back. I begged and prayed to be allowed to stay with them, but they said, 'No, you must go back; and if you do not go willingly, we will make you go.' I cried and tried to stay, but they drove me back, even beating me when I stopped and would not go on. So I was driven over the road I had come, back through all those happy people. They were still joyous and happy, but when they saw that I was not allowed to stay, they turned on me."

She walked for sixty miles, back through the villages, until she reached her home and stood by her body again.

"I looked at it and hated it. Was that my body? What a horrid, loathsome thing it was to me now, since I had seen so many beautiful, happy creatures! Must I go and live in that thing again? No, I would not go into it; I rebelled and cried for mercy.

"'You must go into it; we will make you!' said my tormentors. They took me and pushed me head foremost into the big toe.

"I struggled and fought, but could not help myself. They pushed and beat me again, when I tried for the last time to escape. When I passed the waist, I seemed to know it was of no use to struggle any more, so went the rest of the way myself. Then my body came to life again, and I opened my eyes."

Creepy Crawlies

Bugs, spiders, insects, arachnids, the order Hemiptera, four legs or six, wings, no wings, yackkety yack ... I could go on about the scientific classifications, but you know what? Let's keep it simple. If a creature makes you shriek and yell for your dad to bring a paper towel, it's in this chapter. Is it something you smack with a shoe or a magazine? It's in this chapter. Do you swat it while it's biting your arm? It's in this chapter. There. Simple. Except roaches. They are so disgusting; I put them in a chapter all to themselves.

Can you see this letter ☞ C right here? That's the size of a grown bedbug. These teeny bloodsuckers love to snack on us humans.

Bed Bugs

"Good night, sleep tight, don't let the bedbugs bite," was a silly little nursery saying for a long time. Because after about 1940, no one had bedbugs. Thinking about them was kind of quaint and old fashioned. But after decades away ... they're back! That's for several reasons: different pesticides in use; people traveling on planes way more than they used to, which lets the bugs spread around the globe; and, modern doctors didn't even know what a bedbug bite looked like when they saw one. In the past few years, people have realized that bedbugs are back among us. The race to get rid of them is back on!

© Roy Chang

Weird, but true
Trained dogs can help exterminators find bedbugs by sniffing them out.

Bedbugs hide in beds—on the headboard, under the mattress, with their flat bodies pressed into crevices. Then at night, they come out to feed. They usually bite people on their heads or necks, but will also gladly glom into arms and legs. It takes them about two to five minutes to feed; as they suck, their bodies become round and red as they fill up on blood. They waddle back to their hiding nook. As they digest, over the course of about a week, they become flat again—all the better for hiding under the pillow!

© MorganOliver | Dreamstime.com

Bedbugs are found all over the world, and hitch rides in suitcases and on clothes. In Hawai'i, they can be found in hotels, airlines, cruise ships, homes, restaurants, dorm rooms ... they just want to be near people, and usually stay within eight feet of their feeding area. While they love to hang out in beds, they can also be found underneath wallpaper or under chipped paint on walls, along the walls or ceiling, in sofas and chairs, or in your belongings, like backpacks, books, stuffed animals and clothes.

Creepy bedbug fact
They can live for months without a meal if they have to, just waiting for a host to feast on. Bedbugs will also bite cats and dogs.

Myth, debunked! Did a mall in New Jersey really have to close due to bedbugs? Nope. Just an Internet rumor.

How do you know if you have an infestation of bedbugs?

❶ You go to bed normal, and wake up with red, itchy bites, or break out in a rash.

❷ You spot little black splotches on your bed (this is bedbug poop).

❸ You pull away the bed frame and are horrified by a clump of adults, eggs and shed skins. If this doesn't have you run out of the room screaming, I don't know what would!

© Ralf Kraft | Dreamstime.com

Secret weapon against bedbugs: Vacuums! They suck 'em up. Hotels are supposed to have a designated vacuum in case they get an infestation.

Bees

Special delivery! Did you know the Big Island helps supply the whole world with queen bees? It's true. Companies here raise queen bees and sell them to farmers, who need bee colonies to help pollinate crops like blueberries, apples and almonds.

400,000

That's how many queen bees get sent from Hawai'i to the Mainland each year.

How do they get there? They are shipped via U.S. mail, express service, or via airmail.

© Roy Chang

How many of these bee facts do you know?

❶ Honeybees don't put pollen in their stomachs; they use a special sack in their abdomen and keep it separate.

❷ To make one pound of honey, bees have to tap two million flowers. The hive will cover 55,000 miles to make that one pound of honey!

❸ Unlike a queen bee, a worker honeybee only lives about thirty-five days.

❹ A bee can fly two miles to get food, but going that far wears out their wings. They prefer to get food closer to home.

❺ Honeybees have four wings. ▄ ▄ ▄ ▄ ➡

⑥ Bees go back to their hives at night, or, if the weather is bad.

⑦ What are those huge black bees you see in Hawai'i? Carpenter bees. They aren't dangerous, but are a nuisance since they dig holes in wood to use as nests—they can weaken the roof of a home, dig into a utility pole or wreck a shed. Male carpenter bees can't sting, but are famous for "dive bombing" at people. The females are shyer, but can sting.

⑧ You've heard of beeswax, but have you heard of propolis? This is made by bees using plant resin and can be collected from their hives. It's used to make toothpaste and chewing gum!

⑨ Bees collect more pollen than they need, so beekeepers can take the excess pollen and sell it for use in shampoos, conditioners and body lotion.

⑩ After several unsuccessful tries, honeybees were finally brought by ship to Hawai'i in 1857, arriving on O'ahu. Earlier shipments of bee colonies had gotten too hot on the ships, melting the honeycombs and killing the bees.

⑪ If you're ever near a swarm of bees, the best thing to do is hold still or very slowly walk away. Don't start swinging your arms around or swatting at them. An angry bee can chase you for several miles!

Big-Headed Ant

If your friend is getting all full of himself, use this fancy word on him: megacephala. That means "big head."

Big-headed ants originally came from Central Africa, but now they are on a permanent vacation in Hawai'i. Why? Because they love hanging out near pineapples. Pineapple growers do not, however, love them back, because the ants chew holes through the irrigation tubes. And, they spread diseases all around the pineapple field.

© Gordon Miller | Dreamstime.com

What's weirder:

Honeydew is a melon, true, but the word can mean another thing. When aphids— teensy, sucking insects—or mealybugs are eating, they stick their mouths into a plant. As they suck on the sap, pressure builds up inside them and a sugary goo shoots out their rear ends. That's called honeydew and apparently it's delicious to ants. Some types of ants even "milk" the aphids by stroking them with their antennae, coaxing them to poop out the honeydew. Certain aphids are so used to being milked like little dairy cows that they can't even poop on their own unless there's an ant there to rub them.

What's weird:

Big-headed ants leave piles of dirt or sand around. It's actually their foraging tubes. If you see this in your house, it might mean you have some unwelcome—and messy!—guests.

Weirdest still:
To keep an aphid from escaping, an ant will tear the aphid's wings off so it can keep getting its honeydew fix.

Okay, yuck.
So what's *else* is on the menu?

menu

Peanut butter pet food fruit juice and molasses all appeal to hungry big-headed ants.

Creepy!
Big-headed ants can swarm over much larger animals—like baby seabirds and skinks (a type of lizard)—and eat them. Gulp!

© Photobee | Dreamstime.com

© Roy Chang

When it comes to ants, the Islands lucked out. We have many varieties—forty species. Here are some of the freaky ants of Hawai'i:

❧ When stepped on, odorous house ants smell awful.

❧ Acrobat ants don't smell great, either, and are aggressive. They are called acrobats because they walk along utility lines and fences.

❧ Look under a stone or slab, and you'll find pavement ants. Since they famously enjoy eating pet food, they could also be called Puppy Chow Ants.

❧ Pharaoh ants need a lot of water, leading them to scour for it in wacky places, like aquariums and air conditioners. Who knew you could find ants hanging around your pet fish?

❧ Ouch! Fire ants sting, and if their nest is disturbed, hundreds of them will pour out of it, ready to fight. As if that's not bad enough, fire ants can live in colonies of up to 250,000 ants. That's a whole lot of firepower! The sting from a fire ant can last for weeks and even leave scars. They seem to like banana plants, ti plants and palms.

❧ Do you hear something? Carpenter ants make their nests in wood. If you listen closely, you can hear them chewing through your house. Colonies can be huge—up to 100,000 carpenter ants will live together.

❧ Sneaking up on you… Thief ants like to live close to other species of ants so they can steal their food.

❧ Crazy ants move in jerky, sudden ways, making them look like they are lost or confused.

❧ Spooky ghost ants have pale bodies and like to hide under carpets.

Three Totally Disgusting Fly Facts:

❶ When house flies land on food, they regurgitate whatever food is already in their stomachs to liquefy the new food. Then they slurp it all back up. And worse, they've probably already been eating stuff like dog doo, trash or a dead animal before they visited your potato salad.

❷ Drain flies, also known by the oh-so-cute name of sewer flies, lay their eggs in the muck that lines sink and toilet drains. Their have long breathing tubes that go to the surface so they can breathe air.

❸ Laying their eggs on earthworms, cluster flies give their babies a ready source of fresh, tasty worm meat to eat.

Please eat all you throw up before returning to Buffet.

© Roy Chang

95% of bird mites are females.

© Roy Chang

Bird Mites

Bird mites are tiny parasites that usually live on birds, like mynahs, pigeons or chickens. But if their bird host flies away or dies, they are stuck. Now we have thousands of tiny bird mites, getting hungry. They need a host mammal to feed on, so at dusk, they will head out, in a swarm of thousands, toward the nearest warm body. A rat, a mouse, a cat. Wait, could that body be yours? Yup.

Once bird mites come inside a house, they will get into everything the—into the couch, chairs, clothing, carpet, sheets and blankets. They'll even infest a car! Wherever they are, they hide in tiny crevices, until nighttime, when they come out to feed. On the plus side, they can't live on just humans. We're not their preferred food source and while they will bite us, they won't stay on us long-term.

Bird mites are relatives of spiders and ticks. When they bite you, you'll feel itchy—that's from their saliva—and find small, red bumps on your skin. Unfortunately, these bites take a long time to heal, much longer than a mosquito bite takes to stop itching. The mites are small, so while you might feel them when they are crawling on your body, they are hard to see; only about the size of the period at the end of this sentence.

More facts about these dastardly little critters:

- Mites can slow down their bodies if it gets too hot or cold for them, surviving temperatures as low as minus four! They prefer warm, humid places...like Hawai'i.
- Sometimes infestations get so bad inside a chicken coop, a farmer will have to burn down the whole coop and start over with a new one.
- Ninety-five percent of bird mites are females.
- Mites breathe through their bodies.
- They are rather transparent, which makes them even harder to see, unless they have just fed on blood. Then they look red or black.
- Just like werewolves, bird mites are most active during a full moon.
- Without a blood meal, mites will die within a month or so.

I'm itching just writing this section—is it making you itch to read about mites?

Centipedes

Slithering, lightning fast, across your foot, and just plain horrifying, centipedes seem like they escaped out of some horror movie. Here are ten creepy centipede facts.

❶ It's a myth that they have a hundred legs...they have a mere forty-two legs.

❷ Some centipedes can grow up to twelve inches long. In Hawai'i, they average seven or eight inches.

❸ Prehistoric centipedes grew up to three feet long.

❹ The venomous jaws of a centipede are beneath their heads. Their venom is poisonous to their prey, but not to humans, and they don't tend to bite humans unless they are feeling threatened or got stepped on. Still, their puncture-wound bites are incredibly painful. And if you're allergic to the bite, it can cause major swelling. It would actually take 1,000 centipedes to make enough venom to kill an adult human.

❺ Leave me alone! Centipedes like to be by themselves, in a nice wet, dark spot like under fallen leaves or under a rock. If they get inside your house, they will likely hide in a damp place, like inside your shoe, your closet, or in the bathroom. Since they are nocturnal, they are also known to crawl up into your blankets and sheets while you are sleeping.

❻ What's on the menu? Centipedes are hunters. They like crickets, worms, ants, termites, spiders and flying insects. Bigger species will also eat mice, small reptiles and amphibians.

❼ A centipede can live up to ten years. Unless you get him first!

1829 Was a banner year for Hawai'i, when centipedes and scorpions were both seen in the Islands for the first time.

❽ Unlike a cockroach, which can be whacked to death with a slippah, centipedes are notoriously sturdy. You'll need a big, heavy shoe—at least. The best way to kill one is to chop it into a bunch of small pieces. Don't hack a centipede in half; you'll just have two angry—still mobile—pieces. Some people flush them, other people use tongs to take them outside, stick them down the garbage disposal or back over them with their truck. Hey, whatever works.

❾ They can drop their legs off their bodies if they are threatened, and grow the body part back later. But unlike worms, if you chop one in half, the two halves will not grow into new centipedes.

❿ Several species of centipedes glow in the dark.

© Robstark | Dreamstime.com

Koa Bug

A beautiful green creature speckled with rainbow hues, this is Hawai'i's largest native bug. It looks like a big green leaf, and unlike some of its stink bug relatives, it's a "stinkless stink bug." It is rare, and now found mostly on the Big Island.

Flesh-Eating Caterpillars

A scientist at the University of Hawai'i discovered a kind of caterpillar that eats meat. The caterpillars are so rare, they can only be found on Maui. *Hyposmocoma molluscivora* (try saying THAT fast) crawls along until it finds a slow-moving snail. Then it uses its silk to tie the snail down. Imagine this whole battle taking place in slow motion, and you're at about right—it takes an hour! Then the caterpillar scoots inside the trapped snail's shell and eats it alive.

Koa Looper Moths

These caterpillars and the moths they turn into are found only on O'ahu, Maui and the Big Island. Every once in a while, they get unusually hungry. In spring of 2013, for example, they have been chewing all the leaves off the koa trees near Hilo and Hāmākua, to the tune of 24,500 acres. It's the biggest snack attack the caterpillars have had since 1892, scientists say. During these unusual outbreaks, caterpillars can be seen swarming on the trees and on the ground.

Did You Know?

The University of Hawai'i has an Insect Museum in Mānoa. It has a 225,000 insect specimens! As a research museum, it's for scientific use, but sometimes students are allowed in for special school tours.

Stinging Nettle Caterpillar

This little guy refuses to be like other caterpillars, which are mostly cute, fuzzy and peace loving. Nettle caterpillars are covered in spines, and they are not just for show. They are actually venomous so if you touch the spines, your skin will burn. You might get even have a rash or welts that last for days.

But there's a weapon against this invasive species: a wasp. The parasitic wasp paralyzes the caterpillar by stinging it. Then it lays its eggs right on top of the body of the caterpillar. When those wasp eggs hatch—voila: a handy meal is right there for the wasp larvae to enjoy. Paralyzed caterpillar. Yum, yum! Take that, you nasty stinging caterpillar.

© Jocic | Dreamstime.com

🕷 There are a million and a half species of insects in the world? The U.S. alone has 91,000 species.

🕷 Some ant colonies can have up to twenty million ants.

🕷 The Hercules beetle, a rhinoceros beetle native to South America, can lift 850 times its own weight.

🕷 People feed their pet Goliath beetles dog food.

🕷 Houseflies taste with their feet.

🕷 There are more kinds of beetles than there are of plants.

🕷 Dragonflies zoom along at thir- miles an hour.

© Subbotina | Dreamstime.com

Mosquitoes

Supposedly, mosquitoes were brought to the Islands in 1826 when a bunch of sailors dumped a barrel of water—infested with baby mosquito larvae—near the house of some missionaries they were angry at. The missionaries were making new laws and taking away their fun, the sailors said. That's pretty good revenge, as long as you can sail away!

Here are twenty interesting things about mosquitoes. How many do you know?

❶ Mosquitoes don't technically bite. They use a long, pointed mouthpart, called the proboscis, to pierce into tiny blood vessels near the skin: our capillaries. Inside the proboscis are two tiny tubes: one sucks out the blood, and the other injects saliva, which thins our blood and keeps it from clotting so they can keep slurping away.

❷ The bump you get is an allergic reaction to the saliva.

❸ A "wheal" is the fancy name for a mosquito-bite bump.

❹ You don't have to worry about being bitten by male mosquitoes; it's just the females. Males eat flower nectar. How dainty!

⑤ How do these females find you? Not with their eyes. They can detect the carbon dioxide you exhale in your breath from a long way away. They can also smell our sweat and can sense our body heat.

⑥ They're hard to smack because they can sense movement from eighteen feet away.

⑦ If you eat bananas, you are more likely to get bitten by a mosquito.

⑧ Life is short for a mosquito: about two weeks to six months, tops.

⑨ Their wings beat 500 to 600 times a second.

⑩ If you're wearing dark clothes, you are more likely to get bitten than if you are wearing white or light-colored clothing.

⑪ Mosquitoes spread dengue fever, malaria, West Nile virus, and encephalitis—all diseases that can kill human beings. They are the deadliest creatures in the world, because of the number of people who get sick after being bitten by a mosquito.

⑫ Cannibals! Some mosquito larvae will eat other larvae.

⑬ The reason you can't feel one when it lands on you: It only weighs 1/15,000 of an ounce.

⑭ Humans are on the menu, true, but these hungry little vampires also bite cows, alligators, dogs, horses, elephants, snakes, toads, birds, and cats.

⑮ No one understands why, but mosquitoes seem attracted to perfume, shampoo, and lotion.

⑯ Unless they are in water, mosquito eggs cannot hatch.

...No, No! They have to eat it first.

© Roy Chang

17 Some kinds of mosquitoes like clean water to lay their eggs in; other species actually prefer polluted water.

18 Bzzzzzz... They fly about a mile an hour.

19 One in ten people are particularly attractive to mosquitoes. Theories range on why this is. It might be because a person eats a lot of sugar, or, because they have a lot of cholesterol in your blood. It might even be due to having a certain blood type.

20 If you don't want to get bitten, eat a lot of spicy foods, garlic, and citrus fruits.

Scorpions

Seen far less often than centipedes, scorpions are still found prowling around Maui, O'ahu and the Big Island. They look kind of like miniature lobsters, but they have a long, segmented tail with a sharp, curved tip. That's how they sting and paralyze their prey—and they sting repeatedly, bam, bam, bam! They also have pinchers for grabbing. Even little baby scorpions already have venom and can sting, just like the adults.

Scorpions like to eat at night and dine on insects and spiders; bigger species will even eat small mice or lizards. Scorpions don't eat dead insects; they like the thrill of the hunt and only eat animals that are alive.

© Rpy Chang

Scorpions are usually found near a source of water, like in your kitchen or bathroom, or hiding in a cozy spot, like in your closet, in your shoes or inside folded blankets. My Grandmother once went to take a sip of water out of her mug and looked down to see a scorpion!

The Islands are home to the "lesser brown scorpion," which is not poisonous to humans. In fact, out of 1,700 species of scorpion, only twenty-five have venom that can kill a human. Hawai'i's also aren't huge like some species in other places, where scorpions can grow to up to ten inches long!

And just think: Arizona has forty-five species and we only have one species, so it could be worse. Still, it would be very painful to be stung.

After courtship, the female scorpion will often turn to the male and…eat him.

Scorpions do not lay eggs; they have live babies. The tiny scorpions, called "scorplings" crawl onto their mother's back, and ride around on top of her for a few weeks. There, they are safe until they get bigger. Well, sort of safe. Sometimes, the mama eats the babies. **BURP!**

© Jun Ya Loke | Dreamstime.com

They live a long time, anywhere from three years to thirty, depending on the species. And as a species, they've been on Earth a really long time: 430 million years. Scientists think they were some of the first animals to come on land out of the water. Prehistoric sea scorpions were as big as today's crocodiles, about eight feet long.

These guys are tough!

Researchers have tried freezing a scorpion, then putting it out in the sun, and it just thawed out and walked away. Humans can't do that! Here's another cool trick: Under ultraviolet light, they glow. And, if food is not available, they can slow their bodies down and live on just one meal of an insect for the whole year. Buried under sand, a scorpion can live up to six months without food or water. They can crawl up most surfaces, including walls, but can't climb glass. In places where scorpions are very common, some people put bed and crib legs into mason jars so that scorpions can't crawl up.

Spiders

Many people have a deep, primal fear of spiders. That's called arachnophobia. Luckily, Hawai'i is not home to the world's largest spider, the Goliath Tarantula. It grows to nearly a foot long, and has fangs that are an inch long! It's creepy—but remember, it lives far away from us, in the remote rainforests of South America.

Let's look at some of our homegrown spiders and see how they compare on the scare-o-meter.

© Amwu | Dreamstime.com

VERY SCARY!

Black widows are rarely seen in the Islands. They are venomous and their bite can cause severe muscle cramps, nausea and raised blood pressure. Despite their deadly reputation, black widow venom rarely kills a grown human; only five percent of the bites result in death.

Black widows like to hang out in dark places, like sheds and garages, though you never know: one was found in a bunch of grapes at a Safeway in Hawai'i Kai. One of the unique things about black widows is that they have a telltale, hourglass shaped patch on their undersides that is red or orange. What I want to know is: Who is crazy enough to flip over a spider to check?!

Want to hear something gross? To eat their prey, such as a beetle or fly, a black widow punctures it with her fangs and sticks in digestive enzymes, which turns the inside of the bug to mush. Then she can just suck up the fluid.

Non-aggressive **brown violin spiders** like to hide under boards or tree bark. Still, a bite will cause a blister, fever, chills, shock and on extremely rare occasions, death.

© Photomyeye | Dreamstime.com

We also have to deal with **brown widows.** The bad news is they are more common than the black widows. The good news is they are less poisonous than black widows, though that's possibly just because they are smaller. They like to be left alone, seeking quiet spots like storage closets, unused mailboxes, or under an eave in the garage.

Spider removal tip:

If you use a vacuum to suck up a spider or a spider egg sac, make sure to remove the vacuum cleaner bag right away and seal it in a zip-top plastic bag. Then throw it out. Otherwise, the spiders might come crawling right back out of the vacuum machine. Eek!

KIND OF SCARY!

I once saw a five-inch **cane spider** crawling across the hood of a car. I felt like I was in a horror movie—I wanted to scream out to warn the driver of the car, but my mouth just fell open in horror. And I didn't know the sign language for, "Excuse me, ma'am! There's a *Heteropoda venatoria* trying to take the wheel!"

Actually, cane spiders, otherwise known as the brown huntsman or the giant crab spider, don't attack humans, nor do they try to drive. However, they are still enormous. And hairy.

When a lady cane spider is hāpai, she carries around an egg sac around with her. It's pretty big, about 1.5 centimeters, and looks like a white hockey puck. Inside are 200 baby spiders. (Doesn't that make you want to drop this book and run screaming?) This egg sac makes it hard for her to move around. Otherwise, cane spiders are known for moving incredibly fast; so fast, it seems like they magically reappear in a new place a second later. They don't weave a web, so they have to bust a move to grab their prey, such as cockroaches and silver fish.

Little knubby **crab spiders,** also called **Asian Spiny-Backed spiders,** are found on the Big Island. They are aggressive and if you mess with their web, they will bite you.

Hairy-looking **lynx spider**s use the long spines on their legs to help them catch insects. They have keen eyesight and are great at leaping after their prey.

© Cathy Keifer | Dreamstime.com

Hawaiian Garden Spiders are interesting because the girl spiders are much, much bigger than the boy spiders. The ladies are two to three inches long, with brilliant yellow bodies and boldly striped legs, while the males are brown. Their webs have odd, thick zigzag patterns down the middle of them. Show-offs!

NOT TOO SCARY, BUT STILL...

Most **wolf spiders** have two large eyes in the middle of a row of eight eyes. But because they live underground, in lava caves, Kaua'i cave wolf spiders have adapted to the dark. They have no eyes at all! They are extremely rare, found only in the Kōloa-Po'ipū areas of Kaua'i. The mama spider carries her eggs in her mouth until they are ready to hatch, and when her offspring arrive, they climb up onto her back so she can carry them until they are big enough to defend themselves. To hunt, the spiders use their sense of smell, and then grab their prey, since they do not weave webs.

In Hawaiian, **nananana makaki'i** means "face-patterned spider." These long-legged spiders live in the rainforests of the Big Island, O'ahu, Moloka'i and Maui. Usually bright yellow, they often have what appears to be a big, smiling face on their backs. Sometimes it's so distinct, it looks like someone doodled on them with markers. But that's just how Mother Nature makes them.

Fun word alert! Kleptoparasitism = When one spider steals food from its partner.

Termites

Termites have different jobs, and bodies to match—some are soldiers, others are workers, kings or queens, in charge of laying a lot of eggs. What happens if things get out of balance, and a colony has too many soldiers? No problem: Cannibalism quickly gets things back to normal.

Queens can make 36,000 eggs per day. Kings and queens can live up to twenty-five years. That's an awful lot of grandchildren!

Soldiers defend the termite nest with powerful jaws, snapping off the heads of any invading ants. Other kinds of termites use chemical weapons out of their front glands, shooting out sticky goo that entraps any enemies. Another kind, *Rhinotermes,* even squirts a stinky gas out of its front.

Workers feed all the other termites, transferring regurgitated food into their mouths or by—are you ready for this?—anal feeding. That's where a little drop of special liquid food is produced from the worker termite's anus, and the other termite licks it.

$ FIVE BILLION DOLLARS

That's how much damage to property termites cause each year. Termite damage is more likely to hurt a house than earthquakes, fires or storms.

© Roy Chang

There are roughly **2,000 termite species,** but the worst kind is the Formosan. They are hungry, and aggressive, organizing themselves in huge mud nests inside the walls of a house. And guess which state has got them? Hawai'i! We also have subterranean termites, which live in colonies of up to two million termites.

I built my house of ... The three little pigs have nothing on termites, which build their nest using poop and spit as cement.

© Bevanward | Dreamstime.com

What's on the menu?

Depending on what type of termite, these insects might eat:

menu

fresh wood
decaying wood
fabric made from plants
foam
plastic
tree stumps
wallpaper
drywall
their dead friends
furniture
carpet
and the aforementioned anal goo

Western Yellowjackets

You might think of yellow jackets as annoying pests who come and swarm around your picnic. But western yellow jackets eat a shocking variety of things. A researcher named Erin Wilson studied the wasps on the Big Island and on Maui, collecting food from the jaws of wasps to see what the insects had just eaten. It turns out the yellow jackets scavenge little balls of meat from dead pheasants and other birds; rats; geckos, and other lizards. They will also hunt caterpillars and honeybees, quickly lopping off a bee's head to disable it before they start eating it.

© Vladvitek | Dreamstime.com

What a Horrible Way to Go

There's an old Scouts' song that goes like this:

> "Announcements, announcements, announcements.
> What a horrible way to die, a horrible way to die,
> What a terrible death to be talked to death
> A horrible way to die."

The thing is, nobody actually dies from listening to windbags. But people do die in terrible—and interesting—ways. And I bet you're wondering what some of those might be, yes? Read on.

Ate a Puffer fish

There's enough deadly toxin in one puffer fish to kill thirty grown humans. The toxin is 1,2000 times more deadly than cyanide! If people eat enough of the toxin, by eating the fish's liver, they can die within minutes. First, a person would feel a little dizzy and weak. Then they throw up, get diarrhea, cramps, itchiness, dilated pupils. Then they sink into a type of zombie state, where they are aware of what's happening around them, but cannot move. Then they stop breathing. Worse, you can't reverse this: there is no antidote to the poison.

© Roy Chang

Despite the danger, puffer fish are considered a delicacy in some cultures, such as Japan, Korea, and the Philippines. People like it because it makes their lips a little tingly. In Japan, the fish is called fugu, and fugu chefs study for years to learn how to cut the fish into sashimi without poisoning anyone. They skin the fish while it's still alive and lop off the head. Yum, a pile of sushi served with a still-gasping decapitated fish head! This dish is no laughing matter: a few people die each year from fugu that hasn't been prepared correctly.

© Kwerry | Dreamstime.com

Cannonball Accident

Famous American sea captain and explorer John Kendrick arrived in Honolulu in 1794, back when it was called Fair Haven. He quickly got himself tangled up in a civil war between Kalanikupule, and his half-brother, Ka'eokulani. Kendrick agreed to help Kalanikupule, who won a victory. Toasting his success, Capt. Kendrick's brig, the *Washington*, fired a thirteen-gun salute. A British ship, the *Jackal*, tried to answer back with its own thirteen-gun salute. But whoops! The cannon was supposed to be unloaded, but it was still filled will ammunition. It blasted into the *Washington*, right to the table where Capt. Kendrick was sitting. It killed him and several other sailors.

© Tmorris9 | Dreamstime.com

cracked by a coconut

A man was standing under a coconut tree, when another man tried to kick a coconut down for him. "It struck him squarely on top of his skull; he dropped, and died within a few minutes," writes Canadian doctor Peter Barss, who has studied deaths in the Pacific region. He's also done the reporting on "Grass-skirt burns in Papua New Guinea," and "Penetrating Wounds Caused by Needlefish in Oceania." (For more on needlefish, see the chapter "It Came from the Deep.")

© Roy Chang

Things That Are More Likely to Kill You Than a Shark:

- **450** People die in the U.S. each year from falling out of bed.
- Bathtubs kill **340** people a year.
- Vending machines kill **13** people a year when they topple over onto them.
- Jellyfish bump off **40** humans a year.
- Yearly, **100** people die from getting hit by an icicle, just in Russia alone.
- Hot dogs kill **70** children a year (Chew, people, seriously. And don't give a hot dog to a kid under age three unless it's been cut into teeny pieces.)
- Roller coasters kill **6** people a year.
- Hippos? It turns out they are really dangerous, killing **2,900** people per year.
- Sharks only kill, on average, about **5** humans per year.

Death in Battle

Hawaiian warfare was sophisticated—and deadly. What kinds of weapons did Hawaiian warriors, called koa, use?

- Pikoi, a club attached to a long cord that trips an opponent.
- Throwing axes
- The martial art lua, also called "bone breaking."
- Pahi—daggers embedded with sharp shark's teeth.
- Slippery oil for their bodies, which made them hard to grab by an opponent.
- Swordfish swords
- Rocks flung with a sling.
- Heavy clubs
- Spears
- Pikes—a long spear.

What didn't they use? Metal, which the Hawaiians did not have. After Western contact, the chiefs did buy cannons as well as muskets, a type of gun, and used them.

Fell Into a Volcano

What happens if you fall into a volcano? Scientists have long said that the top of the lava is so dense, you'd stay on the surface. Of course, it's so hot—four times hotter than the broiler of your oven—you'd immediately burn to death. But another researcher recently proved that the gas coming off your burning flesh would quickly change the molten lava, making a hole in it and causing a mini-eruption of lava, called "fountaining." To figure this out, volcano researcher Richard Roscoe filled a sixty-six-pound bag of garbage and filmed what happened when he threw the sack into Ethiopia's Erta Ale Volcano. Here are some other hot tidbits about volcanoes:

Kīlauea is the most active of the five volcanoes that make up the Island chain of Hawai'i. In 1790, it erupted, killing more than 5,000 people on the Big Island. That's the most deadly volcanic eruption in the United States. Mount St. Helens, in contrast, only killed fifty-six people when it blew its top in 1980.

While Kīlauea is one of the most active volcanoes in the world, it is far from the deadliest. **Unzen,** in Japan, claimed 15,000 lives in 1792, for example, while a 1985 eruption of Colombia's **Nevado del Ruiz** killed 25,000. A 1783 eruption of Iceland's **Laki** volcano wiped out a quarter of the whole country and changed the Earth's atmosphere so much, it led to famine world-wide.

A happy ending came for a fifteen-year-old boy who had fallen down twenty-five feet into a crack in the earth at Hawai'i Volcanoes National Park. He had foolishly tried to go over a safety railing near a stem vent and fell in. A rescuer had to rappel down into the ground to get him; the boy was treated for a bump on his head. In 2012, there were twelve search and rescue missions in Hawai'i Volcanoes National Park, and at press time, there have already been seven more in 2013.

Kīlauea started its current eruption in 1983.

© Yann Poirier | Dreamstime.com

Volcanoes kill about **845** humans annually.

Lava can be **2,000** degrees Celsius.

Hawaiians did not sacrifice people into volcanoes.

Kīlauea was particularly active in 1990, when the volcano's lava consumed the Kalapana Gardens neighborhood, Kaimū Black Sand Beach, Mauna Kea Congressional Church, a big section of State Route 130, and Walter Yamaguchi's Kalapana Store.

© Byrnelmogery | Dreamstime.com

F r a g i l e lava can give way. Lava looks sturdy from above, but isn't always supported, or solid, underneath. For example, two people died in 1993 while at the Kīlauea eruption site, when a lava "shelf" gave way. Another woman fell through a lava tube and crashed down thirty feet, breaking both her legs. Forty people died there between 1992 and 2002, but fatalities have been decreasing with newer safety measures in place.

© Golyna Andrushko | Dreamstime.com

What's It Like to be in a Volcanic Explosion?

Here's Ruy Rinch's account of the 1924 eruption of Kīlauea, from the U.S. Geologic Survey:

> 10:36 a.m. Large puffs of steam; rumbling, earthquake. ... Numerous quakes and rumbling. ... A wave of increased air pressure that decidedly hurt my head, was felt at 11:09 a.m. Jumped and exclaimed, "Here comes a terrible one." The air pressure was felt several seconds before rocks appeared and two or three seconds before the explosion cloud cleared the rim. Started to take picture but saw rocks of great dimensions high in the air headed toward our locality. Ran to cliff and slid down a wash. A rock, judging from its air appearance to have weighed over 300 pounds cleared the cliff.
>
> O. Emerson in the afternoon reported a 10-ton rock on airplane landing field while searching for possible killed or wounded soldiers. Two men were seen on rim of pit a short time before 11:09 a.m. explosion. ... Went back to find missing man."

They found the missing man, Taylor. One foot was missing; his other leg shattered and his hands were burned from wiping hot lava off himself. The shoe with his foot still in it was later found. He was cheerful, but died that night at Hilo Hospital.

The gas from a volcano is deadly, too. In 2000, park rangers found the bodies of a man and woman. They had died from inhaling hydrochloric acid, a toxic gas that can form when hot lava hits seawater.

To ancient Hawaiians, a natural death was when someone very old "withered up and flattened out like a lauhala mat."

© Marek Poplawski | Dreamstime.com

Landslide

Eight people died, and fifty were injured, during a landslide at Sacred Falls in 1999, when rocks and boulders came shooting down a dry waterfall bed. The debris was going seventy to one hundred miles an hour and landed in the pool at the base of Sacred Falls. The scary thing is: No one knows why the rockslide started. It hadn't been raining; there was no earthquake. Apparently, many landslides happen without any warning.

Sacred Falls © Douglas Peebles

Slipped In the Tub

Hilo pharmacist Charles Wetmore was known for being an ingenious type. In July 1879, he set up the first telephone line on the Big Island. He also put in a big bathtub—a true luxury at the time—that filled up with cool, refreshing water from a brook near his home. Alas, he came home one day to find his dear wife Lucy had hit her head and drowned in the bathtub.

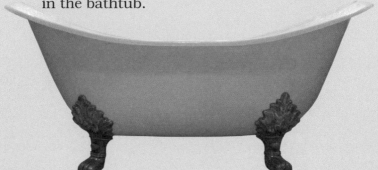

© Nomadsoul1 | Dreamstime.com

Sucked Into the Sweet Stuff

You have probably seen the chimney of an old sugar mill as you go past Kualoa Ranch. It was from the Kualoa Sugar Mill, started in 1865. Sadly, in 1866, the young son the owner, Samuel Wilder, died when he fell into a vat of boiling sugar syrup and was badly burned. William Wilder was only nine years old. The mill closed in 1870; there simply hadn't been enough rain in those years to grow sugar cane on O'ahu.

© Leigh Anne Meeks | Dreamstime.com

Other Weird Sweets-Related Deaths

✿ It was an unusually warm day in Boston on January 15, 1919, when suddenly, a tank exploded. And what came out of the tank? About two and a half million gallons of molasses. A wave of molasses twenty-five feet high poured out, traveling at thirty-five miles an hour. It nearly derailed a train and swept over the neighborhood, killing twenty-one people.

✿ Sugar is still dangerous: In February 2013, a man died falling into a sugar hopper at CSC Sugar in Falls Township, Pennsylvania.

No one was killed, but drivers were injured when two trucks crashed, spilling 8,000 pounds of chocolate on the I-78 highway in 2006. The chocolate was en route to the Hershey plant but wound up all over the road, causing massive traffic delays. If only a truck had come by with some peanut butter, we could have really had something!

Toilet Bowl Washout

At Hanauma Bay's Toilet Bowl, also called "Queen's Bath," is notorious for causing back and neck injuries, as well as drownings. Water is pushed through a hole in the rocks—and rapidly sucked back out. Another "Queen's Bath," in Princeville on Kaua'i, has also been a place many people are injured or drown. If ocean conditions are right, it's a lovely pool. If they're not, churning waves can suddenly knock you off the rocks, sweep you into the ocean, and push you violently back against the rocks. At least 29 people have drowned there.

© Island_images | Dreamstime.com

Plunging off the toilet... England went through a weird spell in 2008, when six people were hurt and one died, falling off a toilet. People injured suffered from back and head injuries, and it was later found that the type of toilet seat was faulty.

© Ib64 | Dreamstime.com

© Roy Chang

Turned into a Stone

In Hawaiian myths, people often get turned into stones by angry gods. Here's what might get you turned into a stone:

- Looking at a naked lady.
- Denying giving Pele a chicken.
- Being the son of a mo'o.
- Whispering during a thunderstorm.

Wacky Worldwide Deaths

Hawai'i isn't the only place weird things happen. These causes of death are so bizarre, they're worth a mention:

☠ You think graduates get a lot of lei around their necks? Well, ancient Greek politician Draco was supposedly smothered by all the cloaks his admirers heaped onto him.

☠ Picky, picky. Novelist Sherwood Anderson died after accidentally swallowing a toothpick at a party. Another famous writer, Tennessee Williams, choked on the cap of his eye-drop bottle when he put it in his mouth and tipped his head back to apply his drops.

☠ Inventor and chemist Thomas Midgley, Jr. strangled when he got caught in the ropes of one of his inventions, a pulley bed. He was the inventor of Freon, by the way, which made it possible for the mass use of refrigerators.

☠ Wealthy playboy Worth Bingham packed his surfboard across the back seat of his convertible. As he passed a parked car, the board hit it, whipped around and crushed his neck.

☠ The deputy mayor of Delhi fell off his building's terrace as he attempted to shoo away a group of attacking rhesus monkeys.

☠ Bad reception killed former big-league baseball player Bo Diaz, who was crushed by the satellite dish on the roof of his house while he was trying to adjust it.

☠ Famous theater director Margo Jones died after her carpet was cleaned. Someone had spilled red paint on her rug during a party,

© Roy Chang

so the carpet cleaners used a lot of a chemical, carbon tetrachloride, to get out the stain. The fumes killed her.

☠ Rock musician Keith Relf was electrocuted by his amplifier while practicing his electric guitar at home. Musicians and weird deaths go hand-in-hand: Mike Edwards, of Electric Light Orchestra, died when a 1,300-pound bale of hay rolled down a hill and crushed his van.

☠ During a race in Belgium, a bird flew into the face of Formula One race driver Alan Stacey, knocking him out and causing him to crash his car. Another kind of crash did in elderly Edward Juchiewicz, who was killed when his ambulance stretcher rolled away, unattended.

☠ After playing "World of Warcraft," for fifty hours, 28-year-old Lee Seung Seop fell off his chair and died.

☠ Is that an alligator bag? A passenger smuggling a crocodile in his duffel bag got on a flight in the Congo. When the croc wriggled loose, everyone on board freaked out and ran toward the cockpit, knocking the plane off balance. Twenty people died in the crash, but the crocodile survived.

☠ And my personal favorite, Jimi Heselden, the owner of the Segway company, was killed when he drove off a cliff... on his Segway.

© John Kasawa | Dreamstime.com

Chapter Seven

Diseases You Definitely Do NOT Want to Catch

Forget catching "the sniffles," or "a twenty-four-hour stomach virus." The diseases in this chapter make the common cold look like child's play. Some of theses diseases kill you—and quickly—while others just make you feel so awful, you wish you were dead. Learning about them can be gross, even downright disturbing. At the same time, diseases play a huge role in human history. For example, King Kamehameha never invaded Kauaʻi because he was stopped by an epidemic—probably cholera—that made him ill and sickened or killed many of his chiefs and warriors. So within the macabre, there's also some interesting science, and an optimist will count his lucky stars we live in an era of modern medicine. One thing's for certain: after reading this chapter, you will want to jump up and wash your hands with soap!

Dengue Fever

This vicious virus causes chills, fever, vomiting, rashes, and worst of all, terrible pain in the arms, legs and behind the eyes. The pain is so bad, it feels like your bones are breaking, which is why it's also dubbed "break bone fever." There's little to treat it, except rest and Tylenol. Even as patients get better, they are still exhausted for months.

Mosquitoes, particularly the Asian tiger mosquito, spread dengue. Those terrible bugs bite all day, not just in the evening, and don't mind the cold—they have been found as far north as Chicago! Once the mosquito bites a victim, the virus starts to reproduce in the person's blood for four to seven days. Then they will start to feel sick.

© Natursports | Dreamstime.com

Dengue fever had become rare in Hawai'i, not seen since 1944 when a bad outbreak caused 1,200 cases. But dengue returned to the Islands in 2001, sickening 153 people, mostly on Maui. In 2012, an Asian tiger mosquito was found at Honolulu International Airport—a bad sign, since the insect spreads the disease so quickly.

Here's the crazy thing: Dengue fever comes in several forms, and if you get dengue fever once, and later get another kind, you're getting a double whammy and likely to develop the disease's worst form, dengue hemorrhagic fever. It sends a person into shock and kills one in five people who come down with it.

Elephantiasis

This one isn't a problem in Hawai'i, but occurs in nearby places in the Pacific, in Guam, American Samoa, the Cook Islands, Kiribati and Tonga. Also known as lymphatic filariasis, this tropical disease causes a huge swelling of body parts. It's spread blood-feeding insects like black flies and mosquitoes. They carry a larvae, or baby stage, roundworm in their bodies and when the insect goes to bite a person to eat the blood, zoop!, out sneaks the larvae, into the human. Once inside a human, the develop into adult roundworms

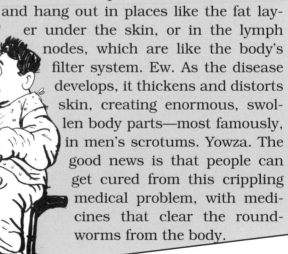

and hang out in places like the fat layer under the skin, or in the lymph nodes, which are like the body's filter system. Ew. As the disease develops, it thickens and distorts skin, creating enormous, swollen body parts—most famously, in men's scrotums. Yowza. The good news is that people can get cured from this crippling medical problem, with medicines that clear the roundworms from the body.

© Roy Chang

flesh-Eating Bacteria!

The real name of this infection is "necrotizing fasciitis," but really, what fun would that be for news anchors to say? It's caused by a bacteria, *Streptococcus*—the same thing that gives people strep throat. Luckily, strep throat is a much more minor problem. It's when the bacteria get further inside your body that it gets really scary: they operate under the skin, sneaking through it, invading the blood system and eating away at the body's fat, muscle and bone layers.

☠ About 1,000 to 1,800 people die each year from flesh-eating bacteria in the United States.

☠ Antibiotics can help treat the infection, but sometimes, doctors have to do surgery to remove the infected body parts. A young woman in Georgia, for example, had both her hands, a leg and a foot amputated to save her life after she came down with flesh-eating bacteria. She'd gotten it through a cut on her leg from a zip-line.

☠ In 2012, three people on Kaua'i came down with flesh-eating bacteria. One of them, Kolohe Kapu, went to the hospital thinking he had a bad case of the flu. But he was actually sick from an infection on his leg. To get all the infected skin and muscle out, doctors had to cut out about a ten-inch-long strip of his leg. "It was about three inches deep and three or four inches wide," his surgeon, Dr. Chris Jordan, told HawaiiNewsNow. Kapu thinks the bacteria got into a small cut in his leg when he was swimming in the ocean off O'ahu.

☠ Bacteria can get into your body through a small cut, but they can even get in through a bruise.

☠ About fifteen to thirty percent of humans have Strep A on their skin and are carrying it around, all the time, without knowing it. It's only a problem, remember, if the bacteria gets into certain places in your body.

☠ Flesh-eating bacteria move so quickly, a small sore on the leg can turn into an infection of the whole leg in just a half hour.

☠ The bacteria can be found in brown or runoff waters, so be sure to take a shower if you go swimming after a heavy rain.

Zoonoses

This is the fancy word for diseases that are spread from animals to humans. Plague is one, and another example is an infection called psittacosis, which people get from pet birds like parrots. Many cats carry bacteria in their mouths, pasteurella, and cats can even give you pink eye! Rats carry about forty diseases that can hurt people, including rat-bite fever, murine typhus, rickettsial pox (yikes, that sounds bad) and Lassa fever.

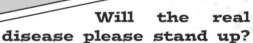

Leptospirosis

Oh look, here's one now! A zoonosis! This disease is spread via animal urine—usually from mongooses or rodents—and can make both people and animals sick.

Lucky you live leptospirosis?

Leptospirosis is much more common in Hawai'i than in other places: the Islands have a rate that's thirty times higher than the rest of the country, with the most cases happening on Kaua'i and the Big Island.

Will the real disease please stand up?

Leptospirosis is or has been called: canicola fever, Weil's syndrome, swamp fever, pseudo-dengue of Java, autumn fever, Rat Catcher's Yellows, Seven-Day fever, Pretibial fever, black jaundice, Fort Bragg fever, cane field fever, and nanukayami fever.

© Yao Zhenyu | Dreamstime.com

Symptoms include fever, chills, headache, vomiting, rash, diarrhea, hearing loss, kidney failure, liver failure and respiratory distress.

Here are some really gross things about this disease:

❶ The bacteria that cause it are contagious as long as they are moist. So if we're talking about bacteria in rat pee, floating downstream... yeah, you can call that moist.

❷ Rats and mice are the most common carriers of the bacteria, but dogs, cows, raccoons, skunks, hedgehogs, rabbits, sheep and deer can all pass along the infections to humans as well.

❸ People usually get it by having infected water splashed into their eyes and nose, like if they jump into a swimming hole or are surfing. Or, through a small cut in the skin. Don't hang out in swimming holes if you have a cut or scrape on you.

© Roy Chang

Measles

Measles causes a rash, high fever, runny nose and cough. It's very contagious—if one person walks into the room with it and starts sneezing or coughing, everyone else is going to get it. You can even get it up to seventy-five minutes after an infected person leaves the room! Children can get a shot to vaccinate them and protect them, but in previous years, this wasn't true.

In 1823, King Kamehameha II and his wife, Queen Kamamalu, traveled to England with a small group of other royalty. They were there to negotiate with King George IV and form an alliance. While touring an orphanage in London, everyone in the group got exposed to the measles—which Hawaiians had no immunity, or natural protection against —and became ill with the disease about a week later. The young king and queen, both only in their twenties, died, and their bodies were brought back to the Islands by a ship.

An 1848 epidemic of the measles hit Hilo first and went on to kill ten to thirty percent of the population. About 150,000 people got the disease, which came in from California that year.

An outbreak in 1984 on Kauaʻi saw 106 children getting measles, and it was traced back to a doctor's office, which hadn't separated sick kids from well ones. Thanks to vaccines, Hawaiʻi now has only one or two cases of the measles each year.

Plague

It's hard to think of a more horrible disease than bubonic plague. Victims get giant boils on their bodies, and their fingertips and toes turn black—that's why this illness is called the Black Death. Blech.

You might think rats spread it, but it's actually spread by fleas. Here's how: a flea bites a sick rat, and then the flea bites a human, transferring the bacteria that cause the disease from the rat to a person. (One more reason to hate rats.) Then the sick human spreads it to other humans by coughing and sneezing.

Bubonic plague's bacteria cause a high fever, gasping breath, horrible headaches, and swellings on the body. It's honestly so vile, and so contagious, I will not go on. It's a terrible way to die, and quick—victims die within a few days, and sometimes even within a few hours. Throughout history, the plague has killed millions of people in Europe. An outbreak in 1890 spread through China, Japan, and India—where it killed ten million people—and finally arrived in Hawai'i in late 1899.

That November, dock workers started to notice that the rats were acting weird, and that they were dying in large numbers. Then people started to notice an unusual amount of dead rats along Nu'uanu Avenue. These dead rats were the first sign of the coming outbreak, which eventually would kill 63 people in Hawai'i in 1899.

For months, the plague was front-page news in the Honolulu newspapers. Who had died and where? You could read all about it. The Board of Health, trying to track the disease, offered a reward of $100 for every real case of the plague reported—that's $2,702 in today's dollars. Downtown—Nu'uanu Street, Maunakea Street, Smith and Pauahi—was a hotbed of plague, so the area was under quarantine. Military guards stood watch outside the houses of people who had been infected with the plague to make sure no one came or went.

Schools were closed. Servants were either not showing up at work, or not allowed to leave their workplace. The mail between the Hawaiian Islands was fumigated to avoid spreading the disease. Chinatown and the wharves were dusted with a disinfectant powder. Outhouses were burned down. The bodies of people who died from the plague were burned in a spare furnace at the Iron Works on Sand Island, as far away from Honolulu as possible.

By January of 1900, the Board of Health started to burn down buildings in Chinatown, trying to get rid of the germs.

Aftermath of the Chinatown fire in 1900, Bishop Museum

But on the twentieth of January, a fire got out of control, and nearly all of Chinatown went up in flames. More than 4,000 people had nowhere to live.

The plague later spread to Hilo and Maui. Three hundred people were quarantined at Camp Wood on Maui because they were suspected of having the plague. By the time the outbreak was over, 337 people had died in Hawai'i. No one died in the terrible fire in Chinatown, though it took months to find houses for everyone.

The last case of plague seen in a person in Hawai'i was on the Big Island, in 1947.

More plague facts

☠ During the worst outbreak of plague in human history, in the years 1346 to 1351, fifty to seventy-five million people died in Europe. That's about a third of the entire population at that time. In some places, it was even worse: Ninety percent of the people of Florence, Italy died.

☠ Today, people can survive the plague if they get treated with antibiotics.

☠ The plague is still a problem in Africa, Asia and South America. It is also seen, though rarely, in California, New Mexico, and Arizona.

Toxoplasmosis

A teeny, tiny, microscopic creature, called a protozoan, is the parasite that causes this disease. Protozoa hang out in the intestines of cats, and get pooped out. If you touch infected cat poop—and in Hawai'i, there are feral cats everywhere—the parasite travels to your brain. It can affect personalities, making people feel sadder, and even cause mental illness. Here's the crazy thing: One third of the people on Earth have these little protozoa in their brains! Eww!

To avoid getting this disease, don't touch cat poop, at home or outside, and don't eat undercooked or raw meat.

Smallpox

Fluid-filled, leaky blisters that then turn crusty... bleeding under the skin—if it sounds horrible, it is. Smallpox is a serious illness that used to kill thousands and thousands of people. Like the chicken pox, a virus, just a different type, causes it. Unlike most of the diseases on our list, it is not spread by animals to humans—just from person to person. Smallpox is very contagious and can spread via saliva, like when someone sneezes. It can also be spread on objects touched by a sick person, like on blankets or sheets.

Smallpox has stalked humans for many centuries; there is even an ancient Egyptian mummy that has the telltale smallpox rash on it. In Hawai'i, the disease first appeared in Honolulu, coming in from San Francisco on a ship in 1853. By July of that year, 4,000 people had smallpox on O'ahu. It caused 1,500 deaths there, then spread to Maui, Kaua'i and the Big Island, killing 450 more people. About eight percent of the whole Island population died during that epidemic.

One of the most famous graveyards was on South Street and Quinn Lane in Honolulu. The Honuakaha Smallpox Cemetery was home to 1,000 burials in 1853 and 1854, all shallow graves that were dug in a hurry. This is near the old Kaka'ako Fire Station, leading to many rumors of hauntings there.

In 1881, another outbreak came to Hawai'i, via passengers on the *Meifoo,* a steamer ship traveling from China. During that outbreak, 789 people got it and 289 died from it.

But there's a happy ending! Vaccine programs helped reduce the numbers of people who got smallpox, until little by little, all over the world, the disease was conquered. The last case of smallpox in the U.S. was seen in 1949, and the very last case of in the world was seen in 1977. Score one for the humans!

Famous world figures who had smallpox: Abraham Lincoln, Joseph Stalin, George Washington, Peter II of Russia, Queen Elizabeth I of England, Ramses V of Egypt, and Chief Sitting Bull.

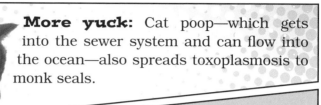

More yuck: Cat poop—which gets into the sewer system and can flow into the ocean—also spreads toxoplasmosis to monk seals.

On the Plus Side

Hawai'i does not have fleas or ticks that give people Lyme disease, or Rocky Mountain Fever, both of which make people sick in other states.

The Islands also never had an outbreak of yellow fever. Two men were diagnosed with it, in 1910 and 1911, but a strict quarantine kept the disease from spreading any further.

Bonus Bizarreness

Haven't had enough strange, icky, wild facts about the Islands yet? Okay, well, hana hou! Here are a few wacky stories that should satisfy any lingering cravings for oddities, gossip, or gore.

Adventures in Sewage

This was a bad chain of events: In 1980, a cane fire on Oʻahu caused an electrical outage of the entire island. Bad enough, but then the pumps stopped working and millions of gallons of raw sewage were dumped into streams, the Ala Wai Canal, and the ocean. Oʻahu got to repeat the fun in 2006, forty-eight million gallons of raw sewage poured into the ocean when a sewer line burst in Honolulu.

Albatross Droppings

You'll never guess how people used to get plants to grow! Yes, one of the early fertilizers used on Hawaiʻi's sugar and pineapple plantations was albatross poop. Or guano, as fancy people like to call bird turds. Half a million tons of the poop was "mined," which is a nice way of describing what must have been disgusting digging work, out of Laysan Island, in the Northwestern Hawaiian Islands. It was shipped into Hawaiʻi for use in agriculture.

© Roy Chang

© Steven Oehlenschlager | Dreamstime.com

Another wacky albatross story: In 2012, a man was driving his pickup truck down the street in Los Angeles when passersby flagged him down and warned him that a large bird was hitching a ride in the back. It was a Laysan albatross from Hawai'i, just chilling, maybe enjoying the So-Cal breeze on its seven-foot wingspan. Scientists think the bird got to California as a stowaway on a container ship—the bird probably landed on it when the boat was at sea and rode all the way to L.A. The driver of the truck turned the bird over to some lifeguards at the beach, and the albatross spent a few days at a wildlife rescue center for observation. It was then released at sea so it could fly back to the Hawaiian Islands. Amazingly, an albatross can fly the whole way back in just a few days, but whether it serves itself peanuts or pretzels midflight remains unknown.

Dogs: It's What's for Dinner

In 2008, two men were arrested in Honolulu for stealing a pet German Shepherd and then eating it. They were sentenced to one year in prison; it's against an animal-cruelty law to kill a dog to use it as a meal.

Babies Galore

Four babies at once! That's called quadruplets, and the first set of them in Hawai'i was born at Tripler Army Medical Center in 1980. Hawai'i actually has a lower rate of multiple births than most other states.

© D. Wesley Enterprises | Dreamstime.com

Angry Ali`i

Ancient Hawaiian rulers, called ali'i, were very strict. If you were a commoner and broke the rules, you might get a bad punishment like getting strangled, or maybe bonked on the head with a big club. Here are the rules you'd have to follow:

The kapu laws were abolished in 1819, by King Kamehameha II.

✗ Your shadow cannot come across the chief's shadow.
✗ Don't touch the ali'i's clothing.
✗ Or his hair or fingernail clippings.
✗ Don't look directly at the chief.
✗ If you're a female, you don't get to eat bananas, coconuts, or pork.
✗ No interrupting the chief when he's talking.
✗ You must observe all the holidays that the chief wants to.
✗ You have to give the chief offerings of food, such as coconuts, fish, and pigs.
✗ Women and men can't eat together in the same place.
✗ You can't set one foot onto land that belongs to an ali'i.
✗ During the summer, only the ali'i can eat the aku fish.
✗ If the chief is eating, you have to kneel down.

© Roy Chang

John Lennon's Killer Was Here

Mark David Chapman, the disturbed man who fatally shot famous Beatle John Lennon, lived in Honolulu in the late 1970s. He worked in maintenance at Castle Medical Center—where he may have previously been a psychiatric patient—and fellow workers called him "an all-around good guy." According to the *Star-Bulletin*, Chapman then got a job as a security guard in Waikīkī. He bought a handgun on Young Street about six weeks before he used it to kill Lennon, on December 8, 1980. On his last day at work as a security guard for the Waikīkī condominium, on October 23, 1980, he signed out the hours log in a very creepy way. He wrote his name as John Lennon.

Justice Served

Don't mess with District Judge Lono Lee. After a man caused a ruckus in his courtroom, breaking a flagpole in half and swinging it around, Judge Lee was understandably annoyed. Judge Lee leapt into action, knocking the man down and putting him in a chokehold until security officers could help out. The man was carted off to Oʻahu Community Correctional Center, and charged with disorderly conduct, obstruction of government operations, and fourth-degree property damage.

Over in Līhue, Fifth Circuit District Court Judge Frank Rothschild heard an unusual case. A woman was accusing her own lawyer of licking her ear and making weird sounds. Judge Rothschild, who called the Kauaʻi-based lawyer a "dirty old man," found him guilty.

© Roy Chang

Lost Camera Case, Closed

A tourist named Lindsay Scallan was visiting Maui in 2007. She was scuba diving when she lost her camera, which was in a waterproof case. Eight years later, the camera washed up on Taiwan's east coast—and the memory card still had the pictures intact and viewable. No one knew whose camera it was, so the photos were posted online to find the camera's owner. Sure enough, Scallan's friend spotted her photos and alerted her that camera was safe and sound. Now, China Airlines has offered Scallan a free trip to come and pick up her camera in person in Taiwan.

© Brad Calkins | Dreamstime.com

Bonus Floating objects

After the tsunami in Japan in 2011, plenty of debris started washing up on Hawai'i's beaches. A seafood storage bin, beer crates, a rusty refrigerator, boats, packages of food, and oyster buoys have all come ashore after spending two years at sea.

Hawaiian Legacy Archives

Shark Ghost

The plan was to build a dry dock for ships in Pearl Harbor. Native Hawaiians warned the U.S. Navy that the dry dock was planned to go over some caves that were the home of Ka'ahupahau and her brother Kahi'uka, guardian shark gods, and that the construction would bother them. Sure enough, when the dry dock was almost done, it collapsed. Engineers blamed it on "seismic tremors," but workers later found the skeleton of a huge shark in the ruins. A kahuna came to bless the area and there were no more problems after that.

Oldest People in Hawai'i

With an average life expectancy of eighty-one years, people in the Islands tend to thrive longer than anywhere else in the U.S. In fact, Hawai'i is fifth in the world for longest life expectancy. So just how old do people get here?

- Elario Questas died at age 112. He'd lived in a rural part of West Maui for a half a century, biked until his nineties, and enjoyed eating rice and sardines. He was born in 1886 and died in 1999—to give you a sense of how old that is, he got a job promotion in 1914.

- A Hilo woman, Take Yazaki, died in August of 2012 at age 108. Florence Shizuko Kamei held the title "oldest woman in Hawai'i" for about a month, dying in September 2012 at age 108. The Kaua'i resident was survived by two great-great-grandchildren!

- The "Gladyator," Gladys Burrell, made the Guinness World Records by running the Honolulu Marathon at age 92.

- An 1896 story in the *Hawaiian Gazette* newspaper profiled Kepoolele Apau, a Hawaiian woman who was supposedly 124 years old. The paper called her a "monument to the past," and noted she had worked as a washerwoman until a fall slowed her down at age 122. Certainly she was ancient but probably not actually THAT old. The oldest person in the world alive today, Jiroemon Kimura, is only 116, and most supercentenarians only live to about 111.

Places to Avoid

☒ Maui's 'Īao Needle has an older name, Kūkaemoku, that translates to "broken excrement." Gee, I wonder why they changed that name?

☒ Molokai's Hahaeule hill. It's name means "tear the penis." Ouch.

☒ Ma'ino, near Hāna, on Maui, has a cliff called Palipilo, or stinking cliff, because it was a dumping ground for human feces.

☒ Papakāhulihuli, a stone in the Wailuku River. If you step on it, it flips over and dumps you into a pit, where you would die. Unless you were clever enough to find your way out through an underground opening.

☒ Popoi'a, just off Kailua Beach Park, literally means "fish rot."

☒ Look out! Pu'upueo, in Mānoa, means "rolling sweet potato hill."

☒ 'Umi, a street in Honolulu. It means "strangle."

☒ Waihe'e on Maui, named for "squid liquid." A giant squid was killed here and "slime flowed over the land," hence the name.

Wiggly Highway

The H2 highway has a weird zigzag pattern of concrete. Supposedly, drivers should not stare at this because they will become disoriented.

It says to turn left after passing Squid Liquid...

© Roy Chang

Stinky Termite Treatment

The Honolulu Brewing and Malting Co. building, on Queen Street, underwent a restoration in 1996. But then the exposed wood areas were treated against termites, the building smelled so bad, no one ever moved in.

The Fugitive

In December of 2012, Justin Wynn Klein allegedly pushed a Japanese visitor off a cliff on Kaua'i's North Shore. She fell fifteen feet but survived, and after a week in the hospital, she returned home to her family. Klein escaped the crime scene and went on the lam for four months. It was thought he might have fled the Islands, but he was on Kaua'i the whole time, supposedly living off goat meat in Kalalau Valley while hiding from the county, state and federal officials who were searching for him. He even took trips to Walmart on the bus for supplies, without anyone noticing.

ENTERING
**TSUNAMI
EVACUATION
AREA**

Tsunami

Hawai'i gets a tsunami about once every twelve years. They happened in 1837, 1841, 1868, 1869, 1872, 1877, 1883, 1906, 1918, 1923, 1933, 1946, 1951, 1952, 1957, 1960, 1975, and 2011. Tsunamis have killed more people in the last century than any other natural disaster.

The 1868 tsunami hit the south end of the Big Island with a sixty-foot wave and caused a landslide that buried a whole village. A 1975 tsunami caused the land near Halapē, also on the Big Island, to sink twelve feet down. A huge hunk of land pulled off; you could see the coconut trees sticking up out of the water. One of the waves from the 1975 tsunami traveled 300 feet inland! On May 23, 1960, a tsunami hit Hilo Bay, shoving boulders that made up the sea wall and moving them 500 feet. A ten-ton tractor was pulled out to sea as the thirty-five-foot waves pushed over buildings and killed sixty-one people.

Tsunami waves travel between 425 and 500 miles an hour. Sometimes the waves hit all at once, but the waves can crash onto land hours apart, too.

Want to read more about the gross and interesting things in this book—or just be sure I wasn't making stuff up? Check out these cool places to learn more.

Cockroach Sources

http://www.asktheexterminator.com/cockroach/Cockroach_Facts.shtml
http://www.pestworldforkids.org/cockroaches.html
http://www.orkin.com/cockroaches/
http://www.sandwichisle.com/pest-identification/profile/cockroaches
http://www.scientificamerican.com/article.cfm?id=fact-or-fiction-cockroach-can-live-without-head
http://www.bio.umass.edu/biology/kunkel/cockroach_faq.html
http://www.uri.edu/ce/factsheets/sheets/cockroaches.html
http://www.wisegeek.com/how-should-i-kill-cockroaches.htm
http://insects.about.com/od/roachesandmantids/f/cockroaches-nuclear-bomb.htm
http://blogs.scientificamerican.com/a-blog-around-the-clock/2011/10/31/revenge-of-the-zombifying-wasp/
http://www.whatsthatbug.com/2011/11/07/emerald-cockroach-wasp-turns-cockroaches-into-zombies/
http://www.cnn.com/2013/03/16/us/greyhound-bus-roaches
http://www.huffingtonpost.com/2011/11/13/charlotte-couple-sues-air_n_1090910.html
http://discovermagazine.com/2007/jan/cockroach-consciousness-neuron-similarity#.UW8oukRrfbs
http://usnews.nbcnews.com/_news/2012/10/10/14343815-death-of-cockroach-eating-contest-winner-in-florida-puzzles-experts?lite
http://www.miamiherald.com/2012/11/26/3114359/man-who-died-during-roach-eating.html
http://www.squidoo.com/i-hate-roaches
http://www.stretcher.com/stories/05/05jun06a.cfm#.UW8v8ERrfbs
http://www.ca.uky.edu/entomology/entfacts/ef614.asp
http://en.wikipedia.org/wiki/Cockroach_racing
http://pestcemetery.com/weird-roach-facts/
http://www.roachcom.net/rofacts/
http://www.youtube.com/watch?v=3QI8XmbdAYc
http://www.saudiaramcoworld.com/issue/199304/cultures.and.cockroaches.htm
http://www.lifeslittlemysteries.com/2296-chocolate-allergies-cockroach-parts.html
http://www.keepinginsects.com/cockroaches-locusts-ants/cockroaches/
http://www.backyardchickens.com/t/344455/hawaii-has-roaches
http://www.planetcockroach.com/cockroach-anatomy.html

It Came from the Deep Sources

Barracuda
http://www.essortment.com/beach-first-aid-identifying-treating-bites-stings-sea-creatures-37819.html
http://www.mauioceancenter.com/index.php?id=11&ss=0&page=marine&content=ma

rine_detail&cat=1&CRid=73&limitstart=0
http://archives.starbulletin.com/97/07/14/news/oceanwatch.html

Box Jellyfish
http://web.utah.edu/umed/students/clubs/international/presentations/dangers.
    html
http://www.hanauma-bay-hawaii.com/jellyfish.html
http://www.dnr.sc.gov/marine/pub/seascience/jellyfi.html
http://animals.nationalgeographic.com/animals/invertebrates/box-jellyfish/
http://www.aquaticcommunity.com/jellyfish/box-seawasp.php
http://eol.org/pages/200766/details
http://www.jyi.org/issue/the-blob-that-attacked-waikiki-the-box-jellyfish-invasion-of-
    hawaii/
http://www.808jellyfish.com/

Cone shells
http://www.marinelifephotography.com/marine/mollusks/gastropods/cones/cones.
    htm
http://pamelakinnairdw.hubpages.com/hub/Cone-Shells-of-Hawaii-Highly-Poisonous
http://therightblue.blogspot.com/2009/04/conus-striatus-fish-eating-cone-shell.html

Cushion Star
http://www.hawaiisfishes.com/books/hawaiis_sea_creatures/creature_samples.htm
http://www.boydski.com/diving/photos/seastars/cushion_star.htm

Eels
http://www.hawaiianencyclopedia.com/eels.asp
http://www.meandmephoto.com/Underwater/Hawaii/Pages/Eels/InfoEels.html
http://www.hanaumabaydivetours.com/photos/hawaii-eels.html
http://blog.stevenwsmeltzer.com/marine-organisms/moray-eels/
http://www.hanauma-bay-hawaii.com/morayeels.html

Flying Fish
http://www.staradvertiser.com/columnists/20100927_Flying_fish_more_plentiful_dur-
    ing_summer_than_winter.html?id=103843178
http://www.susanscott.net/OceanWatch2003/feb07-03.html
http://animals.nationalgeographic.com/animals/fish/flying-fish/

Giant Squid
"In Search of Giant Squid" Curriculum Guide, grades 5-8. The Smithsonian.
http://tolweb.org/tree?group=Architeuthis
http://www.illusionssportfishing.com/squid_large.htm
http://animals.nationalgeographic.com/animals/invertebrates/giant-squid/
http://www.unmuseum.org/squid.htm
http://deepseanews.com/2013/03/23-species-giant-squid-or-just-1/
http://seawifs.gsfc.nasa.gov/OCEAN_PLANET/HTML/squid_Architeuthis.html
http://www.nhm.ac.uk/nature-online/species-of-the-day/collections/our-collections/
    architeuthis-dux/morphology/index.html
http://www.tonmo.com/science/public/giantsquidfacts.php
http://eol.org/pages/488790/overview
http://ocean.si.edu/giant-squid
http://www.smithsonianmag.com/science-nature/The-Giant-Squid-Dragon-of-the-
    Deep.html
http://www.npr.org/2012/03/15/148694025/just-how-big-are-the-eyes-of-a-giant-
    squid
http://www.youtube.com/watch?v=sMZ4dgCjc9E

http://www.cbsnews.com/2100-205_162-592194.html
http://www.sacred-texts.com/pac/hloh/hloh25.htm

Lionfish
http://www.deathtolionfish.org/facts.html
http://animals.nationalgeographic.com/animals/fish/lionfish/?source=A-to-Z
http://www.tfhmagazine.com/details/articles/stings-of-the-scorpaenids.htm

Marine Worms
"Hawai'i's Unearthly Worms," National Geographic, by Jennifer S. Holland, 2007.
Videos at http://ngm.nationalgeographic.com/2007/02/hawaiian-worms/worms-
    video-interactive

Mysterious Purple Crabs
"Millions of tiny purple crabs invade Hawai'i," Fox News, July 17, 2012.
http://www.hawaiinewsnow.com/story/19039793/thousands-of-crabs-wash-up-on-
    oahu-beaches

Manta Rays
http://www.enchantedlearning.com/subjects/sharks/rays/Mantaray.shtml

Needlefish
Know Your Fishes In Hawai'i, by Wilfred Toki. 2005 BeachHouse Publishing.
http://the.honoluluadvertiser.com/article/2005/Jul/30/ln/507300340.html
http://archives.starbulletin.com/2005/07/30/news/story4.html
http://en.wikipedia.org/wiki/Needlefish

Oarfish
http://www.sportfishingmag.com/blogs/next-cast/what-giant-silver-fish-found-float-
    ing-hawaii
http://www.seasky.org/deep-sea/oarfish.html

Octopus
http://marinebio.org/species.asp?id=553
http://www.mauioceancenter.com/index.php?id=11&ss=0&page=marine&content=ma
    rine_detail&cat=2&CRid=31&limitstart=0
http://www.thecephalopodpage.org/
http://eol.org/pages/593207/overview
http://www.sharkfriends.com/wacky/octopus.html

Parrotfish
http://www.marinelifephotography.com/fishes/parrotfishes/parrotfishes.htm

Peacock Flounders
Know Your Fishes In Hawai'i, by Wilfred Toki. 2005 BeachHouse Publishing.
http://www.vetmed.vt.edu/education/curriculum/vm8054/eye/FLOUNDER.HTM

Salps
Dr. Pat Krug, "Take Two" radio program, aired on KPCC March 20, 2013.
http://science.kqed.org/quest/2012/07/03/ocean-overrun-with-gentle-gelatinous-
    salps/
http://goodheartextremescience.wordpress.com/2010/01/27/meet-the-amazing-salp/
https://www.whoi.edu/oceanus/viewArticle.do?id=79766
http://usnews.nbcnews.com/_news/2012/04/27/11432974-diablo-canyon-nuclear-
    plant-in-california-knocked-offline-by-jellyfish-like-creature-called-salp?lite

Sea Anemones

http://www.susanscott.net/OceanWatch2001/mar26-01.html
http://www.flmnh.ufl.edu/malacology/invert.htm
http://www.essortment.com/beach-first-aid-identifying-treating-bites-stings-sea-creatures-37819.html

Sea Cucumbers

http://maukamakai.wordpress.com/2009/09/03/cool-critter-sea-cucumber/
http://www.hawaiisfishes.com/inverts/cucumbers/neatcukes.htm
http://echinoblog.blogspot.com/2012/01/sea-cucumber-evisceration-defense.html
http://echinoblog.blogspot.com/
http://animals.nationalgeographic.com/animals/invertebrates/sea-cucumber/
http://www.fao.org/docrep/007/y5501e/y5501e08.htm

Sea Horses

http://www.sharkfriends.com/wacky/seahorse.html

Sea Slugs

http://www.seaslugforum.net/showall/glauatla
http://seaslugsofhawaii.com/
http://slugsite.us/bow/nudi_han.htm
http://www.newscientist.com/blogs/shortsharpscience/2013/02/sea-slug-penis.html
http://www.foxnews.com/science/2013/02/12/hermaphrodite-sea-slug-mates-with-throwaway-penis/
Place Names of Hawai'i, Mary Kawena Pukui, Samuel H. Elbert and Esther T. Mookini. Copyright 1974.

Sea Urchins

http://www.enchantedlearning.com/subjects/invertebrates/echinoderm/Seaurchin.shtml
http://www.aquariumofpacific.org/onlinelearningcenter/species/red_sea_urchin

Sharks

http://deepseanews.com/2011/09/shark-siblingicide/
http://animals.howstuffworks.com/fish/shark-pup2.htm
http://hawaiisharks.org/aumakua.html
http://hawaiisharks.org/quiz.html
http://daveearley.hubpages.com/hub/Monsters-And-Strange-Creatures-of-The-Earth
http://www.hawaii.edu/himb/sharklab/research/kajiura.html
http://www.sharks-world.com/what_do_sharks_eat.html
http://www.sciencekids.co.nz/sciencefacts/animals/shark.html
http://science.howstuffworks.com/zoology/marine-life/shark4.htm
http://science.howstuffworks.com/zoology/marine-life/shark7.htm
http://adventure.howstuffworks.com/shark-attack1.htm
http://marinelife.about.com/od/Sharks/f/Do-Sharks-Lay-Eggs.htm
http://en.wikipedia.org/wiki/Egg_case_%28Chondrichthyes%29
http://www.huffingtonpost.com/2012/08/09/shark-week-2012-swallowed-discovery-channel_n_1761521.html
http://facts.randomhistory.com/2009/03/11_sharks.html
http://www.masgc.org/page.asp?id=238

Squid

http://www.sharkfriends.com/wacky/squids.html

Tunicates

http://en.wikipedia.org/wiki/Tunicate

http://a-z-animals.com/animals/sea-squirt/
http://goodheartextremescience.wordpress.com/2010/01/27/meet-the-creature-that-eats-its-own-brain/

'Uko'a Fishpond
Place Names of Hawai'i, Mary Kawena Pukui, Samuel H. Elbert and Esther T. Mookini. Copyright 1974.

Whale Poop
http://io9.com/5931648/this-is-what-blue-whale-poop-looks-like-from-an-airplane-tremble
http://carlifrenneman.hubpages.com/hub/This-Is-What-Whale-Poo-Looks-Like

Curious Critters Sources

Axis Deer
http://www.hawaii247.com/2012/10/28/hunters-encouraged-to-help-control-axis-deer/
http://en.wikipedia.org/wiki/Chital
http://hawaiitribune-herald.com/sections/news/local-news/man-convicted-axis-deer-case-feels-unjustly-targeted.html
http://www.venison.com/axis.htm

Bufo Toad
The Hawai'i Bathroom Book, John Richard Stephens. Mutual Publishing. Copyright 2012.
http://www.instanthawaii.com/cgi-bin/hawaii?Animals.bufo
hilo.hawaii.edu/academics/cafnrm/.../ToadpoisoningPDF.pdf
http://en.wikipedia.org/wiki/Cane_toad

Coqui Frogs
http://www.honolulumagazine.com/Honolulu-Magazine/June-2012/Coqui-Frogs-Are-Coming-to-Oahu/
http://candy.about.com/od/candyglossary/a/What-Is-Citric-Acid.htm
http://www.hawaiiinvasivespecies.org/pests/coqui.html
http://online.wsj.com/article/SB10001424127887324883604578399363445540472.html

Donkeys
http://www.humanesociety.org/news/news/2010/09/waikoloa_nightingales_hawaii.html
http://www.conservationhawaii.org/big-island-donkeys-to-be-relocated/

Geckos
http://www.cprofiri.com/content/blogcategory/11/10/
http://holykaw.alltop.com/5-interesting-facts-about-geckos
http://holykaw.alltop.com/5-interesting-facts-about-geckos
http://kids.nationalgeographic.com/kids/animals/creaturefeature/geckos/
http://pets.petsmart.com/guides/leopard-geckos/tips-for-kids.shtml
http://www.accessatlanta.com/news/entertainment/calendar/five-fun-facts-about-geckos-for-geckos-tails-to-to/nQ3qJ/
http://www.explorebiodiversity.com/Hawaii/BiodiversityForgotten/Wildlife/Reptiles/Lizards%20-%20Geckos.htm
http://www.instructables.com/id/How-To-Tame-and-Hand-Feed-Geckos/

Goats

http://www.instanthawaii.com/cgi-bin/hawaii?Animals.goat
http://www.hawaii-forest.com/index.php/articles/feral_goat
http://www.abcbirds.org/conservationissues/threats/invasives/goats.html
http://www.angelfire.com/ak2/blackmask/hunting.html
http://animaldiversity.ummz.umich.edu/accounts/Capra_hircus/
http://pubs.er.usgs.gov/publication/70044212

Feral Chickens

http://www.staradvertiser.com/news/breaking/20130319_Maui_wants_help_to_get_
    rid_of_feral_chickens.html?id=199054511
http://www.npr.org/blogs/thetwo-way/2013/02/28/173163398/in-maui-wild-chick-
    en-spurs-power-outage-at-airport-surrounding-area
http://online.wsj.com/article/SB123863006121980573.html
http://portlandfood.org/topic/11882-feral-chicken-hunt/
http://www.oahuislandnews.com/index.php/feature/comments/one-thousand-years-
    of-wild-oahu-roosters/

Hoary Bat

http://www.fws.gov/pacificislands/fauna/HIhoarybat.html
http://www.earthsendangered.com/profile-533.html
http://www.thewildclassroom.com/bats/hawaiianhoarybat.html
http://www.snopes.com/business/secret/mascara.asp
http://www.to-hawaii.com/fauna.php

Illegal Animals

http://www.hawaiinewsnow.com/story/15159680/illegal-animal-confiscated-in-
    kaneohe
http://www.howtoliveinhawaii.com/2773/bringing-pets-to-hawaii-step-1-prohibited-
    animals/
http://nas.er.usgs.gov/queries/factsheet.aspx?SpeciesID=429
http://link.springer.com/article/10.1007%2FBF00001174
http://www.firefighterclosecalls.com/news/fullstory/newsid/130247
http://mauinow.com/2012/01/25/photos-snake-captured-on-oahu-ferret-found-in-
    hilo/
http://mauinow.com/2012/04/04/live-bat-found-at-honolulus-interisland-terminal/
http://archives.starbulletin.com/98/01/09/news/story5.html
http://www.mauinews.com/page/content.detail/id/527002/6-foot-long-boa-constric-
    tor-captured-in-Big-Isle-garage.html

Mongoose

http://green.blogs.nytimes.com/2012/06/11/an-invader-advances-in-hawaii/
http://www.hawaiiinvasivespecies.org/pests/mongoose.html
http://www.instanthawaii.com/cgi-bin/hawaii?Animals.mongoose
http://www.perlgurl.org/archives/2006/05/the_mongoose_a_maui_menace_1.html
https://sites.google.com/a/hawaii.edu/ndnp-hawaii/Home/historical-feature-articles/
    mongooses
http://blog.sfgate.com/hawaii/2010/02/24/taking-a-gander-at-mongoose-menace/
http://animals.nationalgeographic.com/animals/mammals/mongoose/

Monk Seal

http://www.nwf.org/wildlife/wildlife-library/mammals/hawaiian-monk-seal.aspx
http://www.seaworld.org/animal-info/animal-bytes/animalia/eumetazoa/coelomates/
    deuterostomes/chordata/craniata/mammalia/pinnipedia/monk-seals.htm
http://www.theanimalfiles.com/mammals/seals_sea_lions/hawaiian_monk_seal.html
http://animals.nationalgeographic.com/animals/mammals/hawaiian-monk-seal/

http://www.fpir.noaa.gov/PRD/prd_hms_population_threats.html
http://www.fpir.noaa.gov/PRD/prd_hms_learn_about.html
http://the.honoluluadvertiser.com/article/2004/Aug/27/ln/ln07a.html

Mynah Birds
http://lifestyle.iloveindia.com/lounge/facts-about-mynah-8278.html
http://www.ehow.com/info_8236754_problems-myna-birds-hawaii.html
http://www.mynahbird.org/profiles/manu/manu.html
http://www.sandwichisle.com/pest-identification/profile/other-pest-birds

Nēnē
http://www.arkive.org/nene/branta-sandvicensis/
http://www.instanthawaii.com/cgi-bin/hawaii?Animals.nene
http://www.magical-hawaii.com/Hawaii-State-Bird.html
http://identify.whatbird.com/obj/1103/_/Nene_Goose.aspx
http://srel.uga.edu/ecoviews/ecoview130210.htm
http://www.kilaueapoint.org/education/naturefocus/hnf14/index.html
http://www.ifa.hawaii.edu/info/vis/natural-history/fauna/nene.html

Poi Dog
http://en.wikipedia.org/wiki/Hawaiian_Poi_Dog
http://www.dogbreedinfo.com/hawaiianpoidog.htm
http://books.google.com/books?id=nBzuXFdFECEC&pg=PA139&lpg=PA139&dq=poi+
    dog+Honolulu+zoo&source=bl&ots=9OLJ98Yr68&sig=M2o1HqS0jUGEbU6uDPKr
    GV7_jjw&hl=en&sa=X&ei=Lv52Ucz4C4a0iwKIiYG4Cg&ved=0CEcQ6AEwAw#v=one
    page&q=poi%20dog%20Honolulu%20zoo&f=false
http://www.mauinews.com/page/content.detail/id/519315/MAUI-NEI.html

Rambo
http://www.hawaiinewsnow.com/story/14974024/owner-of-wandering-ram-tracked-
    down
http://www.civilbeat.com/posts/2011/06/01/11366-slideshow-the-ram-living-in-
    aiea/

Rats
U.S. Fish & Wildlife Service, June 2008 fact sheet
http://icwdm.org/handbook/rodents/RoofRats.asp
http://www.ratbehavior.org/Teeth.htm
http://ratfanclub.org/teeth.html
http://www.pestnet.com/rodents/rat-poop/
http://www.pestnet.com/rodents/roof-rat/
http://www.sacred-texts.com/pac/hloh/hloh25.htm

Surprise!
http://news.softpedia.com/news/Rare-Hawaiian-Birds-Spotted-for-the-First-Time-in-
    30-Years-277819.shtml

Wallabies
http://www.hawaiinewsnow.com/global/story.asp?s=10366453
http://archives.starbulletin.com/2007/08/18/news/whatever.html

Wild Pigs
http://www.rarehawaii.org/pigpage/pigs.htm
http://hawaiianforest.com/species
http://archives.starbulletin.com/2003/05/04/news/story2.html
http://www.facts-about.org.uk/facts-about-boars.htm

http://en.wikipedia.org/wiki/Hogzilla
http://abcnews.go.com/GMA/Technology/story?id=599913#.UXRrzURrfbs
http://www.huntwildpig.com/
http://feralhogs.tamu.edu/frequently-asked-questions-wild-pigs/
http://wildpiginfo.msstate.edu/behavior-feral-pigs.html

The Supernatural Sources

Used in Multiple Listings

Asian Supernatural: Including Hawaii and the Pacific, by Alex G. Paman. Mutual Publishing, 2010.
Teller of Hawaiian Tales, Mutual Publishing, 2004 edition.
http://www.carpenoctem.tv/haunted-hotspots/hawaii/
http://www.squidoo.com/haunted-hawaii

Amamanhig

http://maoil.multiply.com/photos/album/26

Bundle Keepers

Haunted Hawaiian Nights, by Lopaka Kapanui. Mutual Publishing, 2005

Castle & Cooke

"Haunted Collector," Season 2, Episode 12. Airs on the SyFy Channel.
http://www.mauinews.com/page/content.detail/id/564465.html
http://www.weirduniverse.net/blog/comments/fijian_cannibal_forks/

Ceiling Licker

http://www.obakemono.com/obake/tenjoname/

Dog-Man

http://www.sacred-texts.com/pac/hloh/hloh17.htm

Egghead Ghost

Glen Grant's Chicken Skin Tales: 49 Favorite Ghost Stories from Hawai'i, by Glen Grant. Mutual Publishing, 1998.

Meet the Ancient Hawaiian Spooks

Hawaiian Legends of Volcanoes, by William D. Westervelt. Mutual Publishing, 1999.
http://www.gohawaii.com/molokai/regions-neighborhoods/east-end/halawa-valley
http://www.sacred-texts.com/pac/hm/hm16.htm
http://www.sacred-texts.com/pac/hlog/hlog26.htm

Going Up?

http://www.honolulumagazine.com/Honolulu-Magazine/Real-Estate/October-2011/Haunted-Honolulu/

Half-Faced Ghost

http://www.weirdus.com/states/hawaii/stories/old_pali_road/index.php
http://www.squidoo.com/haunted-hawaii

Haunted Schools

http://www.hauntedhawaii.net/maui.18.html#MAUI
http://www.strangeusa.com/Viewlocation.aspx?id=2723#sthash.SWp3LKaf.dpbs

How to Revive the Dead
Horror in Paradise: Grim and Uncanny Tales from Hawai'i and the South Seas, edited by A. Grove Day and Basil F. Kirtley. Mutual Publishing, most recent version from 2007.

Images at the Mausoleum
Mauna 'Ala: Hawai'I's Royal Mausoleum. By Don Chapman with WIllaim Kaihe'ekai Mai'oho, Mutual Publishing 2004.

Iao Theater
"Haunted Collector," Season 2, Episode 12. Airs on the SyFy Channel.
http://mauinow.com/2012/08/21/mauis-iao-theater-stars-syfy-channel-ghost-story-episode/#more-75436

Lava
http://www.volcanogallery.com/lavarockIV.htm
http://www.livingmemoriesofmaui.com/lava-rock-plants/the-legend-of-lava/

Military Ghosts
http://voices.yahoo.com/the-top-five-most-haunted-spots-hawaii-diseased-2603827.html?cat=16
http://blainesnutzblog.blogspot.com/2007/03/charley-hickam-air-force-base-ghost.html
http://www.15wing.af.mil/library/factsheets/factsheet.asp?id=5108

Night Marchers
The Hawai'i Bathroom Book, by John Richard Stephens. Mutual Publishing.
http://www.to-hawaii.com/legends/night-marchers.php
http://www.hawaiiweb.com/iliiliopae-heiau.html
Haunted Hawaiian Nights, by Lopaka Kapanui. Mutual Publishing, 2005
http://www.to-hawaii.com/legends/night-marchers.php
Horror in Paradise: Grim and Uncanny Tales from Hawai'i and the South Seas, edited by A. Grove Day and Basil F. Kirtley. Mutual Publishing, most recent version from 2007.
http://blog.hawaii.edu/neojourno/2011/11/28/when-superstition-pervades-logic-and-reason/
http://www.weirdhawaii.com/2008/05/night-marchers-at-kamehameha.html
http://www.unsolvedmysteries.com/usm390878.html

Revenge of the Jilted Bride
http://www.psychicsophia.com/aion/chap8.html

The Woman in the Red Dress
http://www.thingsthatgoboo.com/hauntedplaces/hauntedhawaii.htm
http://www.ehow.com/list_6376263_haunted-hotels-hawaii.html

The Lady in White
Glen Grant's Chicken Skin Tales: 49 Favorite Ghost Stories from Hawai'i, by Glen Grant. Mutual Publishing, 1998.

Thinking to Death
Horror in Paradise: Grim and Uncanny Tales from Hawai'i and the South Seas, edited by A. Grove Day and Basil F. Kirtley. Mutual Publishing, most recent version from 2007.

Tofu Boy
http://hyakumonogatari.com/2012/03/12/tofu-kozo-the-tofu-boy/

Visiting the Other Side

Thrum's Hawaiian Folk Tales, compiled by Thomas G. Thrum. Originally published in 1907; modern edition by Mutual Publishing, Fourth Printing, 2009.

Whistling in the Dark

http://www.weirdhawaii.com/2008/07/whistling-after-dark.html

Who You Gonna Call?

http://www.spookykine.com/

Word to the Wise

The Legend of Morgan's Corner and Other Ghost Stories, by Lopaka Kapanui. Mutual Publishing, 2006.

http://www.psychicsophia.com/aion/chap8.html

Creepy Crawlies Chapter Sources

Intro

http://wiki.answers.com/Q/Is_a_spider_a_bug

Bedbugs

http://www.honolulumagazine.com/Honolulu-Magazine/October-2010/Bedbugs-in-Hawaii/

http://theness.com/neurologicablog/index.php/the-coming-bedbug-plague/

http://bedbugger.com/photos-of-bed-bugs-and-signs-of-bed-bugs/

http://www.nyc.gov/html/doh/bedbugs/html/basics/bed-bug-myths.shtml

http://www1.extension.umn.edu/garden/insects/find/bed-bugs-in-residences/

http://blog.lib.umn.edu/efans/ygnews/2010/11/beware-of-bed-bug-internet-hoa.html

http://www.sandwichisle.com/bed-bugs/bed-bug-education

Bees

http://www.hawaiianqueen.com/pricing.htm

http://www.glenn-apiaries.com/vsh_hawaii_queen_bees.html

http://www.mauinews.com/page/content.detail/id/560484/Queen-bees-king-among-exports-in-Hawaii.html

http://www.foxnews.com/leisure/2010/03/29/secret-lives-beekeepers/

http://www.city-data.com/forum/hawaii/628880-hawaiian-insects-they-really-bad-8.html

http://ento.psu.edu/extension/factsheets/carpenter-bees

http://www.hawaiibeekeepers.org/history.php

http://the.honoluluadvertiser.com/article/2004/Sep/06/ln/ln34ajan.html/?print=on

http://www.captainjohnshoney.com/trivia.htm

Three Fly Facts Sidebar

http://www.idph.state.il.us/envhealth/pcfilthflies.htm

Birdmites.org

http://birdmites.org/index.html

http://birdmites.org/mites.html

http://medent.usyd.edu.au/fact/birdmite.html

http://www.orkin.com/other/mites/bird-mites/

Big-Headed Ants

"Prevention and Control of the Big-Headed Ant," by Glenn Taniguchi, Tommy Thomp-

son and Brent Sipes.
http://entnemdept.ufl.edu/creatures/urban/ants/bigheaded_ant.htm
http://en.wikipedia.org/wiki/Pheidole_megacephala
http://en.wikipedia.org/wiki/Honeydew_%28secretion%29
http://insects.about.com/od/coolandunusualinsects/f/antsandaphids.htm
"Ant Identification Guide," Bayer Environmental Science
http://blogs.scientificamerican.com/extinction-countdown/2012/03/21/blue-tailed-skink-declared-extinct-in-hawaii/
http://westhawaiitoday.com/sections/news/local-news/fire-ants-little-pest-big-problem-invading-isle.html

Centipedes
http://www.hawaii.edu/medicine/pediatrics/pedtext/s21c05.html
http://voices.yahoo.com/are-centipedes-poisonous-hawaii-665640.html
http://voices.yahoo.com/hawaiian-pests-handle-biting-stinging-insects-845777.html?cat=16
http://pamelakinnairdw.hubpages.com/hub/Big-Centipedes-in-Hawaii-Paradise-Anyone
http://www.ecosmartpestcontrol.com/pest_info/centipedes.html
http://en.wikipedia.org/wiki/Scolopendra_subspinipes
http://en.wikipedia.org/wiki/Scolopendra_subspinipes
http://www.extento.hawaii.edu/kbase/urban/Site/Centip.htm
http://www.orkin.com/other/centipedes/how-many-legs-does-a-centipede-have/
http://www.buzzle.com/articles/centipede-bite.html
http://www.uky.edu/Ag/CritterFiles/casefile/relatives/centipedes/centipede.htm
http://www.orkin.com/other/centipedes/fire-centipede/

Flesh-Eating Caterpillar
http://encyclopedia.thefreedictionary.com/Hyposmocoma+molluscivora
http://www.thefreelibrary.com/Meateating+caterpillar%3A+it+hunts+snails+and+ties+them+down.-a0135216756

Koa Caterpillar/Moth
http://dlnr.hawaii.gov/blog/2013/02/14/nr13-013/

Koa Bug
http://en.wikipedia.org/wiki/Coleotichus_blackburniae
http://hbs.bishopmuseum.org/good-bad/koabug.html
http://hbs.bishopmuseum.org/good-bad/koabug-full.html

Did you Know...
http://www.neatorama.com/2007/10/08/the-weirdest-insects-in-the-world/
http://www.si.edu/Encyclopedia_SI/nmnh/buginfo/funfacts.htm
http://www.eastsideexterminators.com/customer-care/fun-facts-for-kids.html

Mosquitoes
The Hawai'i Bathroom Book, John Richard Stephens. Mutual Publishing. Copyright 2012.
http://www.creepycrawlies.info/mosquito-facts.htm
http://www.mosquitomagnet.com/advice/mosquito-info/mosquito-fun-facts
http://www.bestfunfacts.com/mosquitoes.html
http://www.mosquitoworld.net/mosquitofaqs.php
http://insects.about.com/od/flies/a/10-facts-about-mosquitoes.htm
http://animals.nationalgeographic.com/animals/bugs/mosquito/
http://www.webmd.com/allergies/features/are-you-mosquito-magnet

Scorpions
http://beatofhawaii.com/hawaii-centipede-or-scorpion-take-your-pick/
http://www.extento.hawaii.edu/kbase/urban/site/scorp.htm
http://kids.nationalgeographic.com/kids/animals/creaturefeature/scorpions/
http://animalstime.com/scorpion-facts-for-kids-scorpion-diet-habitat/
http://news.nationalgeographic.com/news/2007/11/071121-giant-scorpion.html
http://www.ducksters.com/animals/scorpion.php
http://beautifulandlovely.com/scorpions/

Spiders
University of Florida Institute of Food and Agricultural Sciences
http://entnemdept.ufl.edu/creatures/urban/spiders/giant_crab_spider.htm
http://www.time.com/time/specials/packages/arti-
    cle/0,28804,2092297_2092275_2092278,00.html
http://en.wikipedia.org/wiki/Kaua%CA%BBi_cave_wolf_spider
http://www.thefeaturedcreature.com/2012/03/oh-stop-it-happy-face-spider-youre.
    html
http://www.instanthawaii.com/cgi-bin/hawaii?Animals.cane
http://konacoastpestcontrol.com/Spiders.html
http://animals.nationalgeographic.com/animals/bugs/black-widow-spider/
http://the.honoluluadvertiser.com/article/2003/Nov/29/ln/ln11a.html
http://www.earthsendangered.com/profile-856.html
http://cisr.ucr.edu/brown_widow_spider.html
http://en.wikipedia.org/wiki/Lynx_spider

Stinging Nettle Caterpillar
http://www.hawaiiinvasivespecies.org/pests/nettlecaterpillar.html
http://www.mauinews.com/page/content.detail/id/534059.html

Termites
http://www.pestworld.org/news-and-views/pest-articles/articles/termites-101/
http://insects.about.com/od/termites/a/10-Cool-Facts-About-Termites.htm
http://www.britannica.com/EBchecked/topic/588027/termite
http://link.springer.com/article/10.1007%2FBF00984012?LI=true#page-1
http://entoplp.okstate.edu/ddd/insects/termites.htm
http://www.pestworldforkids.org/termites.html
http://ezinearticles.com/?Learn-Everything-About-What-Termites-Eat&id=656411
http://www.lsuagcenter.com/en/environment/insects/Termites/biology/What-do-
    termites-eat.htm
http://www.sandwichisle.com/termites/ground-termite-control

UH Insect Museum
http://www.ctahr.hawaii.edu/peps/museum/museum_tour.htm
http://www.hawaii.edu/malamalama/2009/10/koa-bug/

Western Yellowjackets
http://news.nationalgeographic.com/news/2009/07/090723-wasps-nests-hawaii.
    html

What a Horrible Way to Go Sources

Ate a Puffer Fish
http://animals.nationalgeographic.com/animals/fish/pufferfish/
http://www.yelp.com/biz/dae-bok-restaurant-los-angeles

http://io9.com/5879406/how-the-puffer-fish-gets-you-high-zombifies-you-and-kills-you
http://www.telegraph.co.uk/foodanddrink/foodanddrinknews/8935973/Two-star-Michelin-restaurant-chef-suspended-over-puffer-fish-poisoning.html
http://scienceblogs.com/retrospectacle/2007/09/25/the-wonderfully-tasty-and-dead/
http://factsanddetails.com/japan.php?itemid=649

Cannonball Accident
https://sites.google.com/site/johnkendrickdar/home
http://www.funtrivia.com/en/subtopics/Unusual-Deaths-No-2-344073.html

Coconut
The Ig Nobel Prizes: The Annals of Improbable Research, by Marc Abrahams. Dutton, copyright 2002.

Died in Battle
http://data.bishopmuseum.org/ethnologydb/type.php?type=shark
http://www.mythichawaii.com/hawaiian-warriors.htm
http://www.ancientmilitary.com/hawaiian-military.htm
http://www.royaltiki.com/Articles/History-And-Culture/The-History-Of-Ancient-Hawaiian-Weaponry
http://www.nps.gov/puhe/historyculture/kamehameha.htm
http://www.wired.com/science/planetearth/multimedia/2008/08/gallery_volcanoes?slide=6&slideView=5
http://www.hawaiihistory.org/index.cfm?fuseaction=ig.page&year=1990
http://hvo.wr.usgs.gov/kilauea/history/1924May18/#conclusions
http://www.earthmagazine.org/article/danger-paradise-hidden-hazards-volcano-geotourism

Things that are more likely to kill you than a shark:
http://www.buzzfeed.com/awesomer/20-things-that-kill-more-people-than-sharks-every

Fell into a Volcano
http://www.huffingtonpost.com/2012/06/27/what-if-you-fell-into-a-volcano_n_1632637.html
http://www.buzzfeed.com/awesomer/20-things-that-kill-more-people-than-sharks-every
http://www.hawaiinewsnow.com/story/21939295/hfd-rescues-boy-after-he-fell-into-lava-tube
http://www.mnn.com/earth-matters/wilderness-resources/stories/death-by-volcano-and-the-physics-of-lava

Old Age
http://www.sacred-texts.com/pac/hm/hm25.htm

Landslide
http://landslides.usgs.gov/recent/archives/1999sacredfalls.php

Prison Riot
http://www.hawaiihistory.org/index.cfm?fuseaction=ig.page&year=1980
http://news.google.com/newspapers?nid=2209&dat=19800607&id=LJ8rAAAAIBAJ&sjid=SvwFAAAAIBAJ&pg=3522,1226789
http://www.prodeathpenalty.com/lwop.htm

Slipped in the Tub
Big Island History Makers, by LaRue W. Piercy. Mutual Publishing. New edition first printing, 2007.

Sucked in the Sweet Stuff
http://science.howstuffworks.com/life/human-biology/10-ways-to-die.htm#page=7
http://www.wired.com/science/discoveries/news/2009/01/dayintech_0115
http://www.ghosttowns.com/states/hi/sugarmillruins.html
http://missionhouses.org/manuscriptfinding/wilder.html
http://articles.mcall.com/2006-04-05/news/3676275_1_truck-chocolate-spill
http://www.kualoa.com/about/history/

Toilet Bowl/Queen's Bath
http://www.tombarefoot.com/info/Kauai_Beaches_Queens_Bath.html
http://www.telegraph.co.uk/news/newstopics/howaboutthat/3251329/Woman-dies-after-lavatory-seat-accident.html
http://www.sfgate.com/hawaii/alohafriday/article/Hawaii-s-most-dangerous-spots-and-how-to-survive-2350469.php
http://great-hikes.com/blog/queens-bath-incidents/

Wacky Worldwide Deaths
http://en.wikipedia.org/wiki/List_of_unusual_deaths
http://frogstorm.com/?p=791
http://www.mnn.com/green-tech/research-innovations/photos/7-inventors-killed-by-their-inventions/thomas-midgley-jr
http://www.dailykos.com/story/2010/01/26/830326/-Three-Inventions-of-Thomas-Midgley-Jr-the-First-Geoengineer
http://en.wikipedia.org/wiki/Margo_Jones
http://en.espnf1.com/f1/motorsport/story/3838.html
http://www.findagrave.com/cgi-bin/fg.cgi?page=gr&GRid=13873255
http://articles.chicagotribune.com/1990-11-25/sports/9004100071_1_major-league-catcher-bo-diaz-paul-owens-venezuelan-winter-league
http://ultimateclassicrock.com/keith-relf-strange-rock-deaths/
http://ultimateclassicrock.com/mike-edwards-strange-rock-deaths/
http://starcrush.com/tennessee-williams-strange-celebrity-deaths/
http://www.snopes.com/medical/emergent/gurney.asp
http://www.nbcnews.com/id/39781214/ns/world_news-africa/t/crocodile-blamed-congo-air-crash/
http://expressindia.indianexpress.com/latest-news/bajwa-succumbs-to-injuries/230828/
http://articles.latimes.com/2005/aug/29/world/fg-games29

Diseases You Definitely Don't Want to Catch Sources

Intro
http://en.wikipedia.org/wiki/Keeaumoku_P%C4%81paiahiahi
http://www.nps.gov/puhe/historyculture/kamehameha.htm

Dengue Fever
http://www.slate.com/articles/health_and_science/pandemics/2012/12/dengue_fever_in_united_states_breakbone_fever_outbreaks_florida_texas_and.html
http://www.hawaiinewsnow.com/story/17205906/rare-mosquito-found-in-honolulu-prompts-call-to-action

Elephantiasis
http://www.who.int/mediacentre/factsheets/fs102/en/

Flesh Eating Bacteria
http://voices.yahoo.com/four-reported-cases-flesh-eating-bacteria-hawaii-11144686.
html
http://www.hawaiinewsnow.com/story/17196610/another-flesh-eating-bacteria-case-
on-kauai
http://www.cdc.gov/ncidod/dbmd/diseaseinfo/groupastreptococcal_g.htm
http://www.hawaiinewsnow.com/story/18614297/www.hawaiinewsnow.com
http://www.hawaiinewsnow.com/story/17171682/kauai-man-fighting-flesh-eating-
bacteria
http://health.howstuffworks.com/skin-care/problems/medical/flesh-eating-bacteria2.
htm

Leptospirosis
http://www.environmentalhealthnews.org/ehs/news/hawaiian-monk-seals
http://en.wikipedia.org/wiki/Leptospirosis
http://www.cdc.gov/leptospirosis/

Measles
http://www.ncbi.nlm.nih.gov/pubmed/19633516
http://library.thinkquest.org/26802/measles.html
http://www.cdc.gov/mmwr/preview/mmwrhtml/00000455.htm
http://the.honoluluadvertiser.com/article/2008/Feb/17/ln/hawaii802170356.html

Plague
The Hawaiian Star newspaper, December 13, 1899.
The Hawaiian Star newspaper, February 14, 1900.
The Hawaiian Star newspaper, March 3, 1900.
The Hawaiian Star newspaper, March 10, 1900.
http://www.hawaiinewsnow.com/story/5080433/the-black-plague-of-1900
http://www.hawaiiforvisitors.com/oahu/events/chinatown-honolulu-fire.htm
http://archives.starbulletin.com/2000/01/24/features/story1.html
http://archives.starbulletin.com/2000/01/25/features/story1.html
http://archives.starbulletin.com/2000/02/01/features/story2.html
http://web.cn.edu/Kwheeler/black_plague.html
http://www.nlm.nih.gov/medlineplus/ency/article/000596.htm
http://www.messybeast.com/zoonoses.htm

On the Plus Side
http://www.hawaii.edu/medicine/pediatrics/pedtext/s21c05.html
http://www.ncbi.nlm.nih.gov/pubmed/8586549

Smallpox
http://kidshealth.org/kid/health_problems/infection/smallpox.html
https://en.wikipedia.org/wiki/Smallpox
http://www.hawaiihistory.org/index.cfm?fuseaction=ig.page&pageid=165
http://totakeresponsibility.blogspot.com/2012/07/smallpox-epidemic-1853.html
http://archives.starbulletin.com/2007/08/03/business/story02.html
http://archives.starbulletin.com/2002/08/18/news/story1.html

Toxoplasmosis
http://blogs.scientificamerican.com/science-sushi/2012/07/04/toxoplasmas-dark-
side-the-link-between-parasite-and-suicide/
http://www.surgicareofhawaii.com/apps/HealthGate/Article.aspx?chunkiid=22497

Bonus Bizarreness Sources

Adventures in Sewage
http://www.hawaiihistory.org/index.cfm?fuseaction=ig.page&year=1983
http://articles.latimes.com/2006/apr/01/nation/na-hawaii1

Alabtross Guano
http://beihawaii.com/company_info.html
http://www.papahanaumokuakea.gov/education/historic_egg_harvesting_laysan.html
http://latimesblogs.latimes.com/lanow/2012/01/albatross-that-stowed-away-to-los-
    angeles-released-offshore.html#more

Angry Ali'i
Page 15, Hawai'i The Big Island Revealed, Wizard Publications, 2002 edition.
http://www.hawaiichristiansonline.com/spiritual_page_3.html
Malo, David, *Hawaiian Antiquities.* Bernice P. Bishop Museum Special Publication 2,
    Second Edition. Honolulu: Bishop Museum Press, 1951.
http://en.wikipedia.org/wiki/Kapu

Babies Galore
http://www.hawaiihistory.org/index.cfm?fuseaction=ig.page&year=1980

Dining on Dogs
http://archives.starbulletin.com/content/20090715_Penalty_for_killing_dog_includes_
    jail_time

Lost Camera
http://www.huffingtonpost.com/2013/03/26/lindsay-scallan-camera-hawaii-
    taiwan_n_2956222.html
http://www.huffingtonpost.com/2013/01/18/japan-tsunami-debris-hawaii-
    fridge_n_2502019.html
https://www.google.com/#sclient=psy-ab&q=tsumami+debris+Hawaii+from+Ja
    pan&oq=tsumami+debris+Hawaii+from+Japan&gs_l=hp.3..33i29i30l4.1054
    .8762.0.8985.41.37.4.0.0.1.302.3898.23j12j1j1.37.0...0.0...1c.1.14.psy-ab.
    awaZH3ROsp4&pbx=1&bav=on.2,or.r_cp.r_qf.&bvm=bv.47008514,d.cGE&fp=99f5
    e912169ca47e&biw=856&bih=746

John Lennon's Killer
http://archives.starbulletin.com/2000/09/26/news/story3.html
http://nymag.com/news/features/45252/index4.html

Justice Served
http://www.chicoer.com/news/ci_20223232/long-arm-law-hawaii-judge-puts-choke-
    hold-unruly
http://www.cbsnews.com/8301-201_162-57472340/hawaii-attorney-convicted-in-ear-
    licking-case/
http://www.hawaiinewsnow.com/story/19022839/kauai-attorney-accused-of-licking-
    clients-ear

Oldest People in Hawai'i
http://archives.starbulletin.com/1999/02/09/news/story8.html
http://www.healthtrends.org/status_life_expect.aspx
http://www.hawaiinewsnow.com/story/19263202/hawaiis-oldest-person-dies-at-108
http://www.staradvertiser.com/sports/breaking/Hawaii_governor_honors_oldest_
    woman_marathoner.html?id=135319128

http://chroniclingamerica.loc.gov/lccn/sn83025121/1896-12-08/ed-1/seq-1/
http://obits.staradvertiser.com/2012/09/20/florence-shizuko-kamei/

Places to Avoid
Place Names of Hawai'i, Mary Kawena Pukui, Samuel H. Elbert and Esther T. Mookini.
   Copyright 1974.

Shark Ghost
http://www.hawaiihistory.org/index.cfm?fuseaction=ig.page&PageID=323&returntona
   me=Short%20Stories&returntopageid=483
http://www.phnsy.navy.mil/timeline/timeline_1909.html
http://aiwa.americanindiansource.com/pearlharbor.html

Stinky Termite Treatment
http://www.honolulumagazine.com/Honolulu-Magazine/February-2012/Walking-
   Honolulu-Queen-Street/index.php?cparticle=3&siarticle=2#artanc

The Fugitive
http://thegardenisland.com/news/attempted-murder-suspect-justin-wynn-klein-in-
   custody/article_b18d5bd0-9fc5-11e2-a72e-0019bb2963f4.html
http://runningwithcats.wordpress.com/2013/04/16/who-helped-justin-wynn-klein-
   eat-in-kalalau-valley-kauai-for-4-months/
http://www.huffingtonpost.com/2012/12/17/justin-wynn-klein-wanted-_n_2318794.
   html
http://www.hawaiinewsnow.com/story/21902729/kau-police-arrest-wanted-attempt-
   ed-murder-suspect-justin-wynn-klein
http://www.hawaiinewscenter.com/kauai-police-arrest-wanted-attempted-murder-
   suspect/

Tsunami
http://mygeologypage.ucdavis.edu/sumner//Teaching/GEL116f00/tsunami2.html
http://www.hawaiianencyclopedia.com/tsunamis.asp
http://hvo.wr.usgs.gov/volcanowatch/archive/1994/94_05_20.html
http://the.honoluluadvertiser.com/article/2006/Apr/01/ln/FP604010322.html

Wiggly Highway
http://en.wikipedia.org/wiki/Wikipedia:WikiProject_Hawaii/Trivia

Index